POWERMENTOR

Also By Kevin M. LaChapelle

Please God, Don't Let My Badge Tarnish:

One Man's Courage to Take a Stand

PowerMentor

Changing lives, one person at a time!
The Art of Mentoring

Kevin M. LaChapelle
Author of
Please God, Don't Let My Badge Tarnish:
One Man's Courage to Take a Stand

iUniverse, Inc.
New York Bloomington Shanghai

PowerMentor
Changing lives, one person at a time!
The Art of Mentoring

iUniverse books may be ordered through booksellers or by contacting:

iUniverse
1663 Liberty Drive
Bloomington, IN 47403
www.iuniverse.com
1-800-Authors (1-800-288-4677)

Because of the dynamic nature of the Internet, any Web addresses or links contained in this book may have changed since publication and may no longer be valid.

The views expressed in this work are solely those of the author and do not necessarily reflect the views of the publisher, and the publisher hereby disclaims any responsibility for them.

ISBN: 978-0-595-49666-2 (pbk)
ISBN: 978-0-595-49404-0 (cloth)
ISBN: 978-0-595-61200-0 (ebk)

Printed in the United States of America

To my mother who has always inspired me to see the good in others and to have a positive attitude in life. I am forever grateful for the example my mother has always set for me. Mom, thank you for never giving up on me, and always believing in me. I love you Mom!

To Javier Quiroz whose life was snatched from him at the early age of only fourteen. His life is a constant reminder that we are not guaranteed tomorrow, and that we must always strive to help those around us live life to their fullest potential. To all of Javier's friends who have made incredible changes in their lives, I am awed by your desire to have purpose in this life and impact those around you. To Javier's brother Agustin, my right hand man, your ability to lead Javier's friends in the midst of the most devastating experience in your life exemplifies who you are as a person. I am thankful for all of you and look forward to walking through this life alongside all of you.

CONTENTS

Foreword

As founder and President of The Leonard Group, Marty Leonard has been working with business and community organizations since 1997. With his book, The 10 Business Principles, *Marty inspires individuals to learn the universal principles of proper behavior in the workplace. The excitement comes when people recognize that these principles work in the home, school or community environments as well. As a Certified Compliance and Ethics Professional, Marty's life experiences, combined with sharp-witted humor, make learning how to be a better member of society an engaging experience. Marty can be reached at www.leonardgroup.com*

Actions based on a framework of right and wrong are the essence of ethical living. Every society has a framework which constitutes "doing the right thing." It's a model for a fulfilled life within that environment. In the United States, we used the Ten Commandments as the foundation of our Constitution and for two hundred years our leaders used this foundation as the guide for what we considered right and wrong.

Today, with a diverse society and declining societal values, our ability to lead and recognize proper behavior is difficult at best. We've seen an erosion of the traditional family unit, corrupt business leaders and wayward politicians—our traditional sources of leadership and guidance.

Kevin LaChapelle has chronicled his life as a mentor, the impact it's had on himself and those he's mentored. In *PowerMentor*, Kevin shares candidly about the sacrifices, heartache and rewards that come with mentoring another individual. In this book Kevin outlines the unchanging framework we need in order to properly mentor others to that fulfilled life.

Throughout this book, you'll read about individuals that lacked boundaries and guidance in their lives, either by intentional neglect or lack of guidance skills.

Mentoring another individual involves a commitment which will require the discipline of cross-checking everything you do so that your actions stay in harmony with your mission of positively impacting another life to the point that they could then "pass it on."

If successful, your rewards will not be in the form of money, power or status. Your rewards will come quietly and without notice from the very one you made your commitment to.

Steve Gonzales is the Mentor Project Coordinator for the More Mentors for Youth Campaign as well as the Founder and President of Dream Weavers, an outreach program working with junior and senior high youth. Steve also is a nationally recognized speaker for many schools and youth programs working with at-risk youth. He has been working with inner city youth and families since 1983.

If you want to change the world, think small. It sounds so backwards to see how our current society functions. When I think of Kevin LaChapelle I think of a man who started small and later would be responsible for touching so many lives.

As a person who is committed to reaching people on the fringe of society, I have a great deal of respect for Kevin and law enforcement personnel like him. I acknowledge that many times these young people are making decisions that are detrimental to themselves and society. As a young man I made many mistakes and made a mess of my teenage years. I remember being at the wrong end of the law many times. I can't think of one police officer during those years who expressed any type of compassion or who sought to understand me as a person. I probably didn't deserve to be treated with compassion for any reason other than the fact that I was a human being. When I met Kevin, I encountered a man who walked a fine line. A man of integrity who wore a badge; and at the same time still cared about people. He cared about those on the fringe of society. He cared for those who had lost their vision and purpose in life. But not only did he say he cared; he also acted on what he said. He treated fairly those who needed to be arrested and had compassion for those who had been affected by those crimes.

Kevin has always acted in the best interest of the young people he has served. He wanted young people to be served fairly and receive the education that they deserved.

Kevin is one of my true heroes. I witnessed a young man act on what he believed. He wanted to make a difference in society and he took on the responsibilities of wearing a badge. He was a good cop. He thought young people desired a quality education and tried to help in that arena as well. I think the world would be a better place if more of us acted on what we truly believed. We may not always be right, but at least we're in the game. Kevin, thanks for being my friend.

Preface

This book will give you insight into almost twenty years of experience in the field of mentoring others. This book will serve as a guidebook and an encouragement to those who seek the selfless act of mentoring others, or those looking for a mentor to help them.

In this book you will hear from individuals who were mentored when they were young and now lead successful lives as adults. They will share with you what worked for them, and what hindered them.

Whether you are a school teacher, college instructor, religious leader, police officer, probation officer, social worker, manager, youth worker, or parent, this book will equip you to learn how to impact and develop those around you so they can live to their full potential.

The mere fact that you are reading this book gives insight into your love and commitment for others. Few really understand what motivates a mentor. This motivating drive is an intrinsic core value that causes us to strive alongside our mentee, believing in them every step of the way.

Some of the stories you will hear in this book are unbelievable. We are talking about a track record of over fifteen years for many of the individuals who were once involved in street gangs, and now are successful college graduates leading a family. I have been blessed tremendously with maintaining these incredible friendships that have impacted me so much, beyond any words to describe it. In addition, I have witnessed the transformation of countless lives that encourage me everyday and give me hope in mankind, when at times we can find it difficult to believe in people.

If you want to see how easily you can have an impact on those around you, if you want to be inspired by the lives around you being transformed, this book is for you. When you are reading this book, note the similarities in what different mentors have found successful in mentoring others. A few should stand out to you, such as looking for what is right in others rather than what is wrong.

Thirteen year old Brian is a good example of how we can help him focus on what is going right in his life instead of the many challenges he faces. To help Brian visualize his future will be a huge step forward. He lives with his mother and four other siblings in one of the worst neighborhoods in San Diego. While working on a video documentary about gang pressures in his neighborhood, Brian asked if he could be interviewed as well. I told him he could. I asked him, "What do you want to be when you grow up?" He told me he would like to have become a fire fighter, but that he did not think it could ever be possible. He then began to cry. After finishing the video a few days later, I took him to a local fire station. The fire fighters began showing Brian the fire trucks and all of the equipment. I took a picture of Brian standing on the front of a ladder truck. I later had the picture enlarged poster size, and had the fire fighters and our mentors write some encouraging words to Brian. Not only did the fire fighters and mentors present the poster to Brian, they also took him for a ride in the fire truck! What do you think that did to restore Brian's vision for his future? The poster is displayed proudly on Brian's wall as a reminder of what the fire fighters encouraged Brian to do if he wanted to become a fireman. They told him to stay out of trouble, do well in school, and to surround himself with the right people! This innovative approach is what it takes to capture the heart of our mentee. In addition, this experience prompted the fire fighters to reflect on how much they can empower a young person in the community they serve.

Often times I am asked by parents, teachers, probation and police officers, how to help a young person leave the gang life. They are surprised at my response. I tell them to stop focusing on their gang problem, and focus on the young person becoming a productive member of their community. If I focus on the gang ties, the drug addiction, the dysfunction, it makes the problem bigger than the solution. I tell them to stop focusing on the problem and focus on the solution. Never will you see me have a workshop on how to leave the gang life. However, you will see me promote a life learning skills workshop, or a job skills course. Within the framework of what I am teaching, I will integrate messages which will help people leave their negative attributes behind without even naming them. This is perhaps one of the greatest challenges of the twelve step programs such as Alcoholics Anonymous. I am consumed with the alcohol addiction so as to not allow the person to ever escape their weakness. The weekly meetings cause the person to be around people with the same weakness, which perpetuates a vicious cycle disallowing the person to actually change. In this book, we will address these issues among many others.

Often times all we hear are the voices of the critics instead of the voices of the Mentors. So many times I hear well meaning individuals critique those around them. Often the critic is mere jealousy that others are doing something positive while the critic restricts themselves to all talk, no action. Theodore Roosevelt said it best:

> *"It is not the critic who counts: not the man who points out how the strong man stumbles or where the doer of deeds could have done better. The credit belongs to the man who is actually in the arena, whose face is marred by dust and sweat and blood, who strives valiantly, who errs and comes up short again and again, because there is no effort without error or shortcoming, but who knows the great enthusiasms, the great devotions, who spends himself for a worthy cause; who, at the best, knows, in the end, the triumph of high achievement, and who, at the worst, if he fails, at least he fails while daring greatly, so that his place shall never be with those cold and timid souls who knew neither victory nor defeat."*

For anyone needing a resource, most of the stories in this book have a short video which can be viewed at www.powermentor.org and used for inspirational purposes.

Acknowledgment

I have been blessed with incredible friends who always surround me and keep me encouraged. Words cannot describe the love that I feel from those God has placed in my life. From family members, friends and colleagues, I can see exactly why each person was meticulously placed in my life to help me grow and live to my fullest possible potential.

I have seen so many people criticized and put down by others. It is an incredible experience when I have seen those same people get focused in their lives, and then soar like eagles. They have made their critics become irrelevant. Each time I witness a person's life take off, it inspires me to continue to believe in people. It is when we can see the greatness in people that they are able to gain the momentum needed to fly high.

I too have had many critics, and likewise I have had so many great friends and advisors in my life to which I am extremely grateful.

I especially am grate to the many friends, family and colleagues who contributed to this book.

CHAPTER 1

▼

WHAT IS A POWERMENTOR

It never ceases to amaze me how a person can be in such despair, yet when they realize that God has a plan laid out for their life, and they find that someone does believe in them, they soar like an eagle. I remember a time when I was mentored by an elderly neighbor. At the time, I had no idea what he was doing, or why he was investing in me. Only today do I realize the impact he had on me, and how God would use that to stir my heart toward mentoring others.

What does it really mean to be a Mentor? A Mentor is generally defined as a wise and trusted counselor or teacher. This definition can be very vague. Let's take a look at the origin of the word Mentor and where it comes from. The word *mentor* is of Greek origin. Most see a mentor as a role model, counselor, advisor, teacher, challenger, encourager, protector, and friend. The most important component in mentoring is that it must be intentional and requires a personal commitment.

In Greek Mythology, Mentor was the son of Alcumus. He was also a great friend of Odysseus. When Odysseus left for the Trojan War, he commissioned Mentor with the care of his son Telemachus. Odysseus had tremendous trust in Mentor, who had served as the guardian to the entire royal household. Because of Mentor's influence, Telemachus became one of the most loved and trusted leaders of his time.

Socrates (470-399 BCE) was accused of corrupting the youth. Socrates mentored many individuals. He was a stone cutter by trade. Throughout his life, Socrates claimed to hear voices which he interpreted as signs from the gods. Socrates spent much of his adult life in the marketplace teaching others about ethical issues.

He had a passion for exposing ignorance, hypocrisy, and conceit among his fellow Athenians regarding moral questions. He was disliked by most of them. However, Socrates had an extremely loyal following. He was very influential in the lives of Plato, Euclid, Alcibiades, and many others. Socrates is known for and admired by many philosophers for his willingness to explore an argument wherever it would lead as well as having the moral courage to follow its conclusion. Socrates was a true Mentor. He had tremendous influence and therefore was a threat to the establishment. What was the driving factor behind Socrates and his commitment to mentor others, especially in light of the fact that he ultimately paid the price with his life? I am confident you will be able to answer this question on your own after reading this book.

Mentoring relationships have been around for a very long time. For example, in the Old Testament of the Bible, King David had a mentoring relationship with Jonathan. We can follow David's growth as his mentor-peer, Jonathan, introduced him to political leadership. David and Jonathan learned from each other. A true mentoring relationship is an intimate friendship in which both the mentor and mentee grow from each other. No one can ignore the unique and powerful friendship that David and Jonathan experienced. What brought them so close? Probably an effective and deliberate mentoring relationship!

To mentor others, is to influence them causing a specific effect. We all have so much influence on those around us. Most of us never recognize that we can strategically direct our influence for the greatest possible impact in the lives of others. We also must take ownership of the negative influence we have as well. We must recognize that we have influence, and in that influence we must make a conscientious effort to have a positive influence and restrain our negative influence on others.

An effective mentor will be focused on drawing out the full potential of others. A wise mentor will be able to help a person grow in wisdom. A mentor is able to affect and impact in a very different manner than a parent could, primarily due to a parent being required to exert discipline and nurturing, while the Mentor can focus on teaching wisdom and strategy, and being a strong encourager. For the parent, if the discipline is not taught in a fair and consistent manner, it can lead to rebellion. Rules without relationships often lead to rebellion. This is why it is critical for mentoring relationships to be focused with structure and purpose to maximize its effectiveness. A mature mentor will develop the person they are mentoring into self-sufficiency. A mentor with questionable motives will lead a person by their true motive of control and power.

Before we can lead others, we must first know ourselves. What motivates us? What drives us? What experiences do we have that can help others? These are all questions we must address to gain a foundation for our mentoring skills.

For me, I wish for others what I did not have. For example, I did not have a positive father role model. My father did not lead me through life by walking alongside me encouraging me. In fact, it was quite the contrary. My father put me down, was not a good example for his children, and treated my mother poorly. Because of this experience, I now try to be for others what I wish I had had in my life. This is what drives me. For each mentor, the motivation may be different.

Often times the ones that are in desperate need of a mentor have been failed by their family. I asked one of our mentors why families seem to be more intact when the children are young, but in the teen years, the family falls apart. His response was that when kids are young they see their parents how they want to see them. When they become teenagers they begin to see their parents as they really are. When they hit that reality, they begin to drift away from the family in search of someone who will believe in them and lead them.

A mentor must have a heart for others. To illustrate this best, consider this story:

> *Come with me to a third grade classroom ... There is a nine-year-old kid sitting at his desk and all of a sudden, there is a puddle between his feet and the front of his pants are wet. He thinks his heart is going to stop because he cannot possibly imagine how this has happened. It's never happened before, and he knows that when the boys find out he will never hear the end of it. When the girls find out, they'll never speak to him again as long as he lives. The boy believes his heart is going to stop; he puts his head down and prays this prayer, "Dear God, this is an emergency! I need help*

now! Five minutes from now I'm dead meat."

He looks up from his prayer and here comes the teacher with a look in her eyes that says he has been discovered.

As the teacher is walking toward him, a classmate named Susie is carrying a goldfish bowl that is filled with water. Susie trips in front of the teacher and inexplicably dumps the bowl of water in the boy's lap.

The boy pretends to be angry, but all the while is saying to himself, "Thank you, Lord! Thank you, Lord!"

Suddenly, instead of being the object of ridicule, the boy is the object of sympathy. The teacher rushes him downstairs and gives him gym shorts to put on while his pants dry out. All the other children are on their hands and knees cleaning up around his desk. The sympathy is wonderful. But as life would have it, the ridicule that should have been his has been transferred to someone else—Susie.

She tries to help, but they tell her to get out. "You've done enough, you klutz!"

Finally, at the end of the day, as they are waiting for the bus, the boy walks over to Susie and whispers, "You did that on purpose, didn't you?" Susie whispers back, "I wet my pants once too."

Susie was willing to take on the embarrassment so the boy would not have to, she had a true heart for others … That is true and undefiled love for another without expecting anything in return. May God help us see the opportunities that are always around us to do good. Mentoring others is a phenomenal opportunity and the rewards are endless.

The most powerful Mentor is God Himself. If we can mirror His love for His people, we will serve our mentee well.

"The glory of friendship is not the outstretched hand, nor the kindly smile, nor the joy of companionship; it is the spiritual inspiration that comes to one when you discover that someone else believes in you and is willing to trust you with a friendship." --Ralph Waldo Emerson

▼

CHAPTER 2

MENTORING WITH PURPOSE

When we journey into mentorship, we must understand that every little action or decision we make will have some sort of an effect on ourselves and those around us. For this reason, we must be very purposeful in our mentoring relationship.

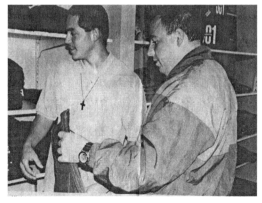

It is crucial that we look for opportunities to teach lessons, instill values, and build up our mentee. For example, I recall a time when I was mentoring a young gang member named Lalo. Lalo was about fifteen years old and was on the road to destroying his life. On one occasion, we went to a movie. While waiting for the movie to start, I asked Lalo if he wanted popcorn, to which he said yes. I gave Lalo my wallet containing cash, credit cards, and my police identification card and told him to order the refreshments and pay for it with the cash in my wallet while I would hold our seats in the movie theater.

More than twelve years later, Lalo is a college graduate and twenty-seven years old. To this day he comments about that incident and how much it impacted him. You will later read about this story from Lalo's perspective. For a police officer to entrust his wallet to him, was just unreal. The profound impact this trust had on Lalo was purposeful, calculated, and strategic. I wanted him to face temptation. I wanted him to reflect on the dilemma of taking something from the one person who was beginning to believe in him. It paid off. We have to be careful, but as we learn to discern, these are masterful moments.

We must realize how many opportunities we will have to plant seeds and teach little lessons. It is similar to the story of the father who was working on a bicycle with his son. A neighbor saw them working tirelessly all day to refurbish the bike. The neighbor told the father that with all of the time he was wasting on fixing the bike, he could easily just go buy a new one. The father replied to the neighbor, "I am not rebuilding a bike, I am building a son!" The reality was that the father was using the refurbishing of the bike as a catalyst in mentoring his son. He was investing in his son, and used the bike merely as a purposeful tool.

Mentoring should not be a routine in which a mentor calls the mentee and invites them to meet with them for an hour every other week. This type of mentoring rarely has impact. This type of mentoring is generally to make the mentor feel like they are doing something good. For example, the commercials we see for big brothers and sisters programs trivialize the role of a mentor. In their commercials the voiceover says, "Think being a big brother takes a lot of time, think again …" The camera then pans to a big brother or sister and their mentee shooting pencils up into the ceiling, or spitting spit wads. Effective mentoring requires a relationship in which the person actually becomes a part of the mentor's life.

Imagine you need some help and go to a counselor. During your session, the counselor continually looks at the watch, and listens to you, but offers little insight or input. After forty-five minutes, a timer bell rings and the counselor immediately stops you dead in your conversation and tells you the session is over and you can pick up next session where you left off. You then walk out to the lobby where you pay for that 45 minute session, feeling the experience was depersonalized. You begin to see that the counselor really has not invested in you. The counselor was merely providing a paid listening session in which you could vent. Here and there the counselor may offer you some insight, but the insight is deficient due to the counselor's not really knowing the full scope of what is happening in your life. The same thing happens when mentoring others. If the relationship is not genuine, and it is more of a chore than a personal commitment, do not expect much impact. What you put into the relationship directly correlates with how successful it will be.

Mentoring is a strategy. For example, every action from you will serve a purpose, so you must plan carefully. For example, I can recall times in which we would have outings during which young people who were not into the gang lifestyle would be drawn to the gang lifestyle because we would mix them all together. We later learned how catastrophic it was and had to begin a classification process for outings. There are two cases where because of our good intentions, young people were fully drawn into the gang life as a direct result of meeting guys that were already in that scene. We also learned how much more effective one-on-one mentoring is compared to group outings. This is not to undermine the fact that there are purposeful times for group outings; however, there must be strategic planning before the outing to discuss any vulnerabilities.

Scope of Influence

Influence is a very powerful tool. It can be used for the good and can be used for the bad. I have learned a great deal over the years about influence and how it must be tempered. Influence can be used manipulatively, which is always self serving; therefore, it has no purpose in productive mentoring.

First I will address some principles that the mentee must quickly learn. One must be very careful as to who is allowed into our inner circle as our support system. Many people, whom we think might be there for us the most, surprise us with great disappointment.

When it comes to influence, we have to have a set of core values that influence our decisions rather than making emotionally based decisions. If we make decisions that are in line or consistent with our core values, rather than allowing people to pressure us with influence, we will find that our decisions are much more solid.

For example, people in general will try and exert influence on those around them. It is our basic human nature to want others to see things as we see them or to want others to be like us. There is a serious danger in this. I find this a lot with religion. Often I come across well-meaning individuals who are so intent on converting others to their specific belief that they fail to help a person grow and find for themselves what truth is.

One of the characteristics I have is transparency. Because I so readily share my flaws with others, friends, including church pastors, political leaders, and many others begin to share things with me that normally people do not trust to share with others. I am careful with my advice because I have a strong level of influence on others. I must temper this for my good as well as theirs. For example, often people want us to make a decision for them so they do not have to take the risk. If the situation later goes awry, they can simply blame everyone else for telling them that was the correct decision.

Over and over I get asked how I am able to have such an impact on those around me. What is your secret, some ask. First of all, you must ask yourself a question. Why try to influence or impact those around you? After all, no one ever tries to influence you—or do they? We all have the opportunity to influence others and likewise be influenced ourselves. The big issue is this: Are you an influencer, or just a person who is influenced? The other issue is this: Do you seek people who have something to offer, or do you seek out people and wonder what you may offer? I choose to see people and dream about their potential for having an impact in this world. The other principle I never forget is this: To have good friends, you must first *be* a good friend!

You may feel that you really do not have that much influence on others, or that others may not necessarily have much influence over you. Consider this: How much does it cost to air a thirty-second commercial, especially during a Super Bowl game? Why? Advertisers know how easily people can be influenced, and how that influence drives sales. If they are willing to spend as much money as they do for a thirty-second slot of influence, imagine what you can do for others by being a positive influence in their life.

Who is in your circle of influence? This term applies to the concept that every person has a "circle" of people around them that they interact with on a regular basis, and whose decisions they can influence. These people include spouses and family, co-workers and friends. The ability for an individual in this circle to affect the decisions made by the others is very strong. Some people surround themselves with 'yes' people. They want everyone around them to agree with everything they say or do. On the other hand, I choose to surround myself with people who are not afraid to challenge me and my beliefs. I have a saying in my office that goes like this: If the both of us agree on everything, one of us needs to go! Iron sharpens iron.

It is also important to share your dreams and vision with those in your circle. You need to become a part of each other's lives. Jesus said it is better to give than to receive. This truth has blessed my life more than I can say. I am blessed with some of the most incredible friendships ever.

You have to overcome the insecurity of demanding a return for your investment in others on your own terms. For example, influencing others can be easily abused. Pyramid schemes are a perfect example. You know the type. You receive a call from that friend of yours you have not heard from in a while. They invite you over for dinner, and, oh yes, they do want to discuss something very special with you. They go on to tell how they have found an incredible opportunity and want to share it with only a few of their most special friends. They are just trying to suck you in. They might also say, "I am so excited as to what I stumbled upon, and I want you to be a part of it too!" When you arrive, they begin to share with you information about their newfound wealth. This is incredibly manipulative. If you abuse friendships like this, you will not only lose friends, but also they will despise you. Anytime you hear dollar signs, you'd better wake up and open your eyes. Anyone trying to influence others for self-gain will become evident, and your true motives will be clear to others.

If you want others to open up to you, you had better be ready to open up to them. People tend to only make themselves vulnerable to those who have made themselves vulnerable as well. For some people this is very difficult. You must take the risk. This is why it is so important for you to determine who you should influence. When you develop a solid support system around you, you will know when it is the right time to open up and share with those around you. Don't forget, to have good friends, you must first be a good friend. If you ever breach that trust, you are doomed to failure in relationships.

After having developed a close relationship with God and sensing a calling in my life to lead others around me, I began to see clearly how much friends can impact each other. I did not feel a calling to lead others as most people define leading, but felt that God would use me to seek out the people in this world that others may see as failures. I always prayed I would be used to motivate them and develop them into becoming strong leaders with character. They would end up being God-driven and be able to resist and deflect tremendous pressure and negative influence from others. That is the purpose God has given to me! I help them prepare themselves to have an enormous impact on this world. If we are not having an impact, than we are irrelevant. Most people desire relevance and purpose in life.

Recently, I was talking to a friend who was having problems with his marriage. He has four young children as well. He felt helpless and purposeless in his life. I told him how men have forgotten what it means to be a strong man. For example, a husband and father must take his role seriously. He had better bring adventure and purpose to his family. A woman wants a man who will lead with purpose and bring excitement to the family. Likewise, kids love excitement and adventure. If the man does not provide this within the family, then his kids will search for it somewhere else. They may find the excitement in street gangs. If you cannot provide this for your wife, she will find the excitement she longs for, with or without you.

A man must have the wisdom to rally the family together for a unified purpose. Whether it is outdoor adventures, helping build homes in Mexico or whatever, the family will thrive on this. Anyone that knows me knows that I always have something going on, and it is always full of excitement and adventure. I do not even have to try. God seems to just open the doors and I choose to walk through them. A  friend of mine told me, "This sounds like too much work." It may be, but what is the alternative—a family full of chaos?

I remember when I performed the marriage ceremony for my brother. After giving a short talk about the role of the family, I was stunned at how many people approached me after the ceremony. They told me of their marriage being on the brink of failure. They told me of all the things they felt they had done wrong. When I told them it was never too late to change, they seemed to find a ray of hope. We seem to forget that tomorrow is the first day of the rest of our life. Surely, we may have consequences from our past inadequacies; however, you would be surprised at how resilient people are. We can never take relationships for granted, as they are the cement for our lives.

A man who has mastered influencing those around him is Steve Gonzalez, founder of Dream Weavers. Steve has been an incredible friend over the years. Steve has a heart for young people like I have never seen before and is probably the most genuine individual I have ever known. His sole purpose is to reach out to young people who do not see hope for their lives. He shows them the love God has for them, and he walks at their side encouraging them to seek God and all he has planned for their lives. When Steve shares success stories with others, it is infectious, and they begin to want to rally around him so he can do more. Steve is definitely a PowerMentor.

CHAPTER 3

▼

CONNECTING WITH OTHERS

Do not talk down to mentees, but rather model a relationship in which you both learn from each other. Be transparent and, as you have purpose in mentoring them, tell them you are equipping them to mentor others as their purpose. Do not make a mentee feel like your pet project. Do not try and take credit for their success. You may have coached them, but the most difficult part is going to be their hard work and tenacity. Do not have high relational expectations. Give without any assumption that you will receive anything in return.

We must focus on seeing and bringing out the good in others instead of constantly focusing on the negative and seeking to destroy those around us. By doing this, those around us will allow their walls to be down, so a relationship can be built. When relationships are built with a proper foundation, they will be able to withstand anything, never allowing anything to come between the bonds of friendship.

An example of this is clearly illustrated with a young man I met when he was 15 years old. His name was Jose Antonio. He was a part of our youth program in the 1990s. This young man was incredible. He had a rough background. He and his mother and brothers grew up in one of the poorest areas of Tijuana. He and I had a tight bond. At one point he went back to Tijuana, but because he did not have legal status to be in the United States, he could not return. I lost touch with Jose Antonio for many years.

On a number of occasions while in Tijuana, Mexico, I tried to locate Jose Antonio to no avail. On one occasion while doing research in Tijuana, I did come across Jose Antonio, who appeared to be homeless and drug addicted, washing car windows on the street. I gave him my phone number and told him to call me, and we would try and help him. He was very low in his life, and it was very hard to see him like this.

For months friends and I tried to find him but were never successful. Finally in 2006, while filming a documentary regarding the correlation of corruption and poverty, I was driving near the busiest intersection of Tijuana called *Cinco y Diez*. While driving, I was telling my colleagues about Jose Antonio and how much I felt we had let him down by not being more assertive with his involvement in our youth program. I told them of how I prayed we could find him to right the fact that we wronged him. While telling them the story, out of the corner of my eye, I see a homeless man who appeared to be similar to Jose Antonio. It had now been ten years since he was in our program, so it was difficult to know for sure if it was him. I rolled down the window and yelled, "Jose," to which he turned and saw me and yelled, "Kevin!" I made a U-turn as soon as I could.

When I pulled off of the road, I jumped out and we embraced like I had never embraced anyone before. He was dirty and smelled bad, but I did not care. How could our lives have moved on with ease, while his life was being destroyed? This was like a prodigal son coming home. We hugged and cried. I told him to come with us. He began sharing that he had always prayed he would find us again one day. He had no means of support from the time he returned back to Tijuana when he was fifteen years old. His mother was in and out of mental institutions, and his two brothers were placed in an orphanage. Because he was too old for the orphanage, he was left to fend for himself.

We went to the store, bought him new clothes, and found a place for him to shower. I will never forget the transformation from when he walked into the bathroom as a stereotypical homeless man. His clothes stunk badly, and he looked rough at a young age of 26. He took a lot of time in the shower trying to clean up. He walked out of the bathroom with his brand new clothes on, and a fresh new look. Of course his skin was worn from the sun, and you could still clearly see he had been through a lot.

I remember one occasion when I drove Jose Antonio from Tijuana to Tecate, Mexico. Jose Antonio was sitting in the back seat. I looked in the rear view mirror and caught a glimpse of tears rolling down his cheeks. He began to weep. I called his name, and he leaned forward. I reach around behind my seat to comfort him, while I pondered the rough road ahead for Jose Antonio.

Later we began to talk about all he had been through. I would learn of his heroin drug use, and the things he had to do to survive on the street. For example, the prostitution, robbing innocent people, and eating out of trashcans filled me with an overwhelming feeling of guilt.

I had to return to San Diego that night. Later in the week, we were able to get Jose Antonio into a drug rehabilitation program. I, along with our lead mentors Agustin and Omar, began the long process of nurturing him back to health and committed to providing him with unconditional love that had been lost for so long. It was a rough few weeks while he was being detoxified from the drugs.

I recall shooting some video of Jose Antonio's story. He wanted to share his story so others could learn. When he revealed some of the most chilling experiences he had been through, Agustin and Omar were right there at his  side. I was filming and had tears running down my face as I saw him share things that would make most people run from him. Instead, Agustin and Omar drew even closer to him, putting their arms around him.

Jose Antonio has now been totally drug and alcohol free for over a year. His body has bounced back phenomenally. He looks like any normal college student. He attends college in the evenings in

Tijuana. The consequences Jose Antonio will face because of his decisions will ultimately cost him his life. During the mentoring portion of our helping him, we conduct weekly drug tests to hold him accountable. While doing the drug tests, we also elected to give him a Hepatitis C and HIV test, for both of which he tested positive. He is not angry at God or anyone. He knows he led a life that could inevitably lead to serious consequences. However, the one thing Jose Antonio continues to be overwhelmed by is the unconditional love and friendship that was offered to him. He acknowledged that when he tested positive for HIV and Hepatitis C, he thought he would never see us again, but he was wrong.

This is the kind of friendship that comes easily for the Power-Mentor. Many people have a defined vision of a mentor as someone who helps others. However, there are many types of mentors. For example, I met an individual while I was in the police academy in 1989. His name was Chris Pietrzak. On September 24, 2007, he passed away from a massive heart attack. I had just spoken to him on the phone the week before, and we were to have lunch the week he died.

Chris was not a dynamic, charismatic individual. Chris was not a great public speaker who spoke out and encouraged the multitudes. It was in Chris' quiet demeanor that a true friend could be found. Chris knew who he was and what he stood for, and there was not any one person that I am aware of who could change that. When reflecting with friends over his loss, it was interesting to hear from almost everyone that Chris never engaged in talking ill of others. Indeed, if you would try and bring up a negative discussion about someone, Chris would just shrug you off and change the subject.

Chris was the kind of friend who stood by you even when others would not. This friendship is so very hard to find, yet for Chris, it came naturally. His smile always seemed to calm the storm and convince you that somehow everything would be okay. His steady personality would be the most consistent thing I would ever know. It was this friendship that sustained me through some of the most difficult times in my life. Many times people underestimate individuals such as Chris. However, I learned very quickly that he knew exactly what he was doing, and he enjoyed knowing that he could be a pillar for his friends. Chris was unmovable. I see Chris as an example of what friendship is all about.

Just when you are awed by people, Jennifer comes along. Jennifer has a terminal illness yet denies herself so she can be there for others. She met Jose Antonio who still has years of life ahead of him, yet she immediately began researching his diseases to see how she could help. All the while, she is not even guaranteed months more to live. Jennifer has many mentors in her life who keep her strong and at the same time, she mentors all who are in her life in her own special way. Here is this heroine's story:

The Jennifer Van Luyn Story
We Are Not Promised Tomorrow So Live For Today

My name is Jennifer Ann Van Luyn. I was born in 1975 in San Diego, California. In 2004, I was diagnosed with Alpha-1 Antitrypsin Deficiency which is a hereditary condition that is passed on from parents to their children through their genes. This condition may result in serious lung and/or liver disease in infants, children and adults.

Alpha-1 occurs when there is a severe lack of protein substance called Alpha-1 Antitypic (AAT) in the blood, which is mainly produced by the liver. The main function of AAT is to protect the lungs from inflammation caused by infection and inhaled irritants such as tobacco smoke. The low level of AAT in the blood occurs because the AAT is abnormal and cannot be released from the liver at the normal rate. This leads to a build-up of abnormal AAT in the liver and can cause liver disease.

Testing for Alpha-1 is quick and accurate. It is done through a blood test or a mouth swab test. The most common symptoms of Alpha-1 relating to the lungs, include shortness of breath, wheezing, chronic cough and sputum, and recurring chest colds. The symptoms related to the liver include eyes and skin turning yellow (jaundice), swelling of the abdomen (ascities), and vomiting blood or passing blood in stools. Symptoms related to the skin include panniculitis.

My mother has been a nurse for twenty-five years, working in an Intensive Care Unit. Due to my illness, I was frequently sick and was having trouble breathing. I had much abdominal pain, skin rashes, and a low platelet count. I was seeing or calling my doctor every week with symptoms. The only thing that resulted from my doctor visits was that I was told I probably had some asthma and was sent home with an inhaler to use. My frequent calls to the doctor's office with a multitude of complaints caused me to be labeled as a nuisance, resulting in a number of altercations between me and the office staff.

Finally, my mom and I sat down with the doctor for a serious meeting. My mom told the doctor, "I realize you believe my daughter is too young to have all of these problems, and her low platelets are normal for her; however, for my own peace of mind, can you do a complete work-up. If you don't find anything, then I will know I did all I could do."

It was at that time that I began having many tests done. I had lab work, painful bone marrow tests, x-rays, CAT Scans, and MRIs. The last test, which was extremely painful, was a liver biopsy. I cannot express the pain I endured.

My mom and I went to my doctor to get all of the test results. It was at this moment that the doctor told us that I had advanced cirrhosis of the liver. He then noted that a previous test for Alpha-1 came back positive. My mom did some research on Alpha-1. After her findings, she looked like someone had just pulled a gun out and killed me. She knew what was in store for me. That's when I realized there was something seriously wrong with me.

It was a tremendous blow to be told I had a rare genetic disease, and that the only information available would be off of the Internet.

No treatment plan was discussed; no further assistance from the doctor was given to us. We just turned around and left the office to devise our own plan of care.

When I was first diagnosed, I think it took my mom and me about a week to absorb everything we had been told and what we had researched up until that point. Every six months I go to my lung doctor, and every two months I go to the liver clinic. I set up monthly appointments with my primary doctor, because my condition is worsening and I need more medications to keep me stable. There is no way of telling how fast my organs are deteriorating.

Two years ago I finally had to stop working. I think that was the hardest thing I ever had to do. Walking out the door of my job for the last time was so hard. I was there for five years to the day. I knew, however, that I could never just sit around and allow myself to die. I knew I had to maintain being an example for my kids. I have a daughter who is twelve and a son who is nine. I had to let them know how important going to school and getting an education is, and how it would help them get ahead in life.

At this point, I decided to attend Remington College. I enrolled for my Associate in Criminal Justice degree. After much hard work I graduated with honors. After finding out I was sick, I had to set more goals for myself. Getting through school was the primary goal.

There is an important fact I need to mention. I believe I am where I am today because of a book I read. I was walking past the office at school and saw a poster advertising a book called, *Please God, Don't Let My Badge Tarnish* written by Kevin LaChapelle. It caught my eye and I called my mom and said, "Mom I have to have this book, can you come and write a check, please?" She brought me the check! It took me only a couple of days to finish reading his book. I never knew who Kevin was, even though I knew he taught at my school. One day I saw Kevin walking to his car as I was pulling out. I rolled down my window and yelled, "Hey Kevin!" He stopped, and I expressed how wonderful his book was. I had just been selected to serve on the San Diego County Juvenile Justice Commission, so I was excited to tell him about it. He told me that it was great, and how much of an impact I could have on the commission. After that day, life has never been the same.

Poor Kevin … Every time I need his help, I call or e-mail him, and he never says no! One day we sat down at Starbucks, his home away from home, and talked about everything. I explained my illness to him. He had all kinds of plans and ideas for me. From that day on, Kevin became a true friend. He gave me more of a reason to live.

A lot has happened from that point in my life. For example, I went to my appointment at the liver clinic and it was the second one I had been to. I will never forget what the doctor said. He explained that to even become a candidate for the liver transplant list, there was a particular scale set by the government. My problem in qualifying was that I can have normal liver functions in the lab tests until the day I die. It was then that the doctor said, "There are special circumstances for filing the form which a doctor can do." In the presence of my daughter, this doctor said, "It is too much paperwork to do something like that." It was then that I left crying. The doctor was so heartless and looked at me as if I were a nobody. Instead of a mother, and a person with children and feelings and a life worth saving, it seemed as though to him, I was an insignificant person. I was trying to assimilate the fact that I had a doctor who felt it was okay that I die.

I also go to a lung specialist. He is very good in treating my condition. He has me on a weekly infusion of a medication called Aralast. This is an infusion that is human-donated Alpha-1 Antitrypsin and it helps protect my lungs. Since I have no decent vein access for weekly infusions, it was at this time I had a port-a-cath, which is a "port," placed under my fatty tissue which has a catheter connected to it and tunneled under the tissue and into a major vein, which eventually enters into my heart. It was placed in the upper right side of my chest. It is the size of a quarter and has rubber in the middle. When I need blood work this port is also used for that purpose. My mom has to access my port at least once a week for my Aralast and I am spared many unsuccessful painful sticks from labs, thanks to my port. When I first had it placed, it was very painful, but now it's better, although I still feel pain from it every once in a while.

The last effect of Alpha-1 is my skin. I get what is known as panniculitis. It is created by an excess of white blood cell products. Panniculitis frequently causes painful lumps under or on the surface of the skin. A person can get them internally and externally. This in itself can also be life threatening when it involves the internal organs. The good thing is, the Aralast infusion helps decrease the panniculitis outbreaks. Fortunately, now I only get them on occasion, although they are more frequent when I am under stress.

Now above all, the most important person to me is my mom. My mom and I have been very close since I was a child. We do everything together. I cannot find the words to explain my mom and what she stands for. I am an only child and have my two kids. We all live with her because she loves having us. My mom has always been by my side. I had a terrible car accident when I was seventeen years old. I was a passenger in the back seat, and an elderly lady ran a red light and T-Boned the car I was in. I had surgery on my stomach and it was left opened, to be packed with gauze so it would close from the bottom up. I broke my left elbow and upper arm. I broke my left femur and have a metal rod in place. My wonderful mom was at the hospital everyday, all day. When I got home she did my nursing care.

With regards to my illness, my mom is an angel, although she feels she is not. I don't know where I would be right now if it weren't for her. My mom, without one complaint, handles all of my care. She makes my bed, and gives me a bath when I am too weak to do it myself. She does my infusions and she controls my medications and administers them to me. When I am too sick, she drives my two kids to and from school at two different schools at two different times. My mom takes my daughter to basketball games and practice, and my son to baseball. On top of all that she works a full-time job.

I get confused sometimes during my "liver flare-ups," and I fire her. I will call her on her pager and tell her to find me a new nurse. I get evil when I'm unable to think clearly, due to my liver. My mom takes all my abuse. I have so many issues, but she puts up with it all. When I cry because the pain is too much, Mom sits by my bed and holds me, crying with me. When I have to endure tests that scare me, she will take time off of work to be there with me. I have a huge phobia with MRIs. She will sit at the end of the machine and hold my head steady, comforting me to ease my claustrophobia. When I need blood work done, she waits with me anywhere from fifteen minutes to an hour. She drives me to all of my doctors' appointments. She will go round and round with doctors, insurance, and the hospitals on my behalf. She never gives up on me. I have a hospital bed in my room with a mattress that I can adjust to my comfort level. In the nights I need to use diapers. I use them because of the diuretics I take, being too sick to get up at times, and falling into deep sleeps.

My mom will lie with me, which always brings a smile to my face. I get major Charlie-horses in my legs to the point they leave bruises. She will sit with me and rub them out until they're gone. My mom knows when I am happy, sad, mad, or glad. There is not one thing this Superwoman won't do for me. At times I don't think my mom realizes how much she does for me. I know that my mom speaks up for me no matter what. She is my life-line. I don't know where I would be right now without her. She takes such good care of me, and the personal things she does for me never ceases to amaze me. I am her life and I know that. I don't know where I'd be right now if she didn't care for me like she does. If I am sick or in the hospital, don't ask her to leave because she will tell you where to go. My mom is very mellow, but when she gets mad, BEWARE! The kids and I tell her that her eyes bulge when she gets really mad. The one thing that makes me so mad is that she never gives herself enough credit. That is why I feel I need to let everyone know who my mom is!

Being a patient with a severe chronic illness, I have witnessed firsthand the problems one must get through within the health care system. I have come to realize that a patient is their own best advocate. We know what works for us and we know what does not. I have very few doctors who will listen to me. I guess they feel like I am out of bounds or maybe they feel I make them look incompetent. That is far from the truth. No matter what your job is, you can always learn. We never stop learning. The question is, who is open to learning? I find that few people are willing to learn. When I go to the Emergency Room, the nurses and the doctors seem not to have a clue. For example, I have my port to allow them to take blood, yet they all still try and use a vein. Most of the time my veins are too fragile and blow when anyone tries to go near them. I try to explain this, but rarely will anyone listen.

The most famous saying I hear is, "Oh, I touched on this Alpha-1 in medical school but I have never dealt with it." When I am given medications, I have to be careful because the doctor at times doesn't consider my illness. What will the consequences be because of a particular medication and the possible side effects? Will it go through the liver and cause further damage. My mom and I look at each other and often try to steer the doctor in the right direction. Because we have been dealing with my illness for a few years now, we are flabbergasted when doctors and nurses insist their way is better, especially when many times, their way has caused me more pain and suffering than if we had done it the way we recommended.

When I first went to a skin doctor before I knew that I had panniculitis, he cut out three pieces of tissue from the sores on my arm, and sent them to the lab. This was on a Tuesday, and the doctor told me to come back on Friday. I did go back on Friday to be sure the samples were sent to the lab. The doctor then told me she wanted another doctor to see the specimens because it was so rare. Three weeks later I received a $500.00 bill! I could not believe that I was charged for something that we did not even ask for. The doctor sent it to the other doctor because of its rarity, and they then send me a bill for that? I hate being used as a guinea pig. It hurts way too much.

On another occasion I had an MRI, and the nurse who was connecting my IV dropped the tubing on the floor after the cap had been removed from the tip. The nurse picked it up and was ready to connect it to my port even though it was no longer sterile. My mom said, "You plan on getting new tubing right?" When the nurse walked away my mom said, "That should have been nursing 101."

As for my faith in God, I have to say for a split second I was mad at God. Why me? What did I do to make God so mad? My mom said, "God is having you save souls." After that I stopped to think, could Mom be right? Now I'm convinced that she is right. She tells me that God needs his special souls to suffer for him to save souls. She said I must be awfully special to share in such an important task for the Almighty God. She tells me that eyes have not seen, nor ears heard, what God has waiting for those who love him. To love Him is to suffer for Him as He chooses. When I am in pain, my mom tells me to offer my suffering to God. So I do. Sometimes I hide how much pain I am in. Someone will ask, "Are you ok? Are you sick?" Many times I won't be honest. The problem is that when my daughter goes with me, she tells these people that her mom is lying, and that I really am in pain.

I have come to terms with my illness. Why should I complain when there are people who are worse off then I am. I refuse to lie in a bed and die. Don't tell me no because I'll do it anyway! God has guided me in the direction I need to go. God has taught me to give to those that don't have. If you do something to get something in return, you are not doing it from your heart. I know I am blessed with God, my mom, my two kids, and friends who care. I myself don't see how a person cannot believe in God. He is number one for me.

My favorite prayer is "Foot Prints". The part I like the most is, "When you only see one set of footprints, it was then that I carried you." At times I get so sick and I offer my suffering to God asking him to please carry me and let up on the pain a little.

God, my mom, my children and Kevin make up my support group. My daughter, Elizabeth, has had to put up with more than a twelve year old should have to deal with as a child. When my mom is working, my daughter takes care of me. She takes my moms place and feeds me. When I need different medications, she knows which ones I need. I often thank her and apologize to her, telling her that she should be doing other things a child should be doing and not taking care of her mom. I cannot express how lucky I am. I know she is going to grow up and be a fine young lady. She already has seen much suffering.

My son, Chris, does his best for a nine year old. He tries to take care of me and I love him for that. Elizabeth is stronger. As for Chris, we tell him it's okay to cry. Chris is a huge mama's boy. He will rub my legs when they are full of water. He will rub my head when my head hurts. My two kids are a true gift from God. I couldn't be luckier.

One person I haven't brought up is my stepdad, Juan. He is involved in the only way he knows how. He would do anything that I asked of him if it meant it would make me more comfortable or live longer. He is unable to be present emotionally because I don't think he can handle it. As soon as he found out I was sick, he bought me a scooter, a lift for my truck, made my house handicap accessible and most of all he got me a hospital bed with a sleep number mattress. Juan is there financially, but he can't handle seeing me sick. He has done so much and I would suffer so much more if it weren't for him.

My advocate, Barbee Bennington, is there in good times and bad. I can call her anytime and she will talk to me for as long as I need. Barbee is one of the people who go to bat for me. If I have a problem, she's there to fix it. If she is unable to fix it, she will find out how to fix it. At one time, I was having a problem with my health coverage and the insurance company stopped my Aralast infusion. Barbee got right on top of it and got me samples to get by until it everything was straightened out. There is not one day that I think she has a bad day, if she does have a bad day, you would never know it. She has become such an important part of my life. I cannot see my life without her.

Lastly, Kevin LaChapelle and I crossed paths and he has been such an inspiration to me. He has no problem speaking his mind. Kevin doesn't put up with any crap no matter who it is. The other thing is, if Kevin is on your side and batting for you, I have to say you are a very lucky person. Kevin has to wear so many different hats and he wears each one well. He is a teacher, is actively involved in grievance groups, SIA, and PowerMentor. Above all, he is a friend who will never let you down.

Kevin and my family have given me the will to keep going. I look at Kevin and he never ceases helping those who are less fortunate.

Chapter 4

▼

Mentor Relationship Skills

As your relationship with your mentee develops, be careful when you begin to see some of your flaws manifest themselves in your mentee. We pass along our negative behaviors as well as our positive personality characteristics.

Your relationship will go through certain mentoring stages. The first stage is when you come across an individual that you feel drawn to. You begin to talk with them and see a vision for that person. During this stage there is apprehension because it is uncertain what direction the relationship may take.

A mentor then has to establish the relationship. It is important for a mentor to establish boundaries or parameters for the relationship. This can be a vulnerable time in the friendship because it is so new. Often times the mentee will feel vulnerable because suddenly there is this person who is taking an interest in them, and they cannot figure out why. In addition, the mentor must be careful so as to not create an environment in which it appears that the mentor wants to make a "project" out of the mentee. We can never forget that mentorship goes both ways. We impact and teach the mentee, and likewise the mentee teaches and impacts us as well. The mentor and mentee should be able to see that they bring out the best in each other. This is how you know you are becoming effective. We must focus on bringing the best out in each other.

The next stage is when the mentor can begin to plant seeds. We first must recognize that if we are mentoring an individual who has been through tough times, often they will be suffering from poor self-worth and low self-confidence. If that is the case, we can begin to plant small seeds of encouragement. When the mentor sees the mentee do something worthy of praise, not only do we praise, but we really affirm the mentee and acknowledge how we see them. For example, a mentee often does not see their potential. If the mentor will point out some of the strengths they see in their mentee, the mentee will start recognizing their talent.

Perhaps the toughest stage in the mentor relationship is the waiting and watching. This is the point in which we must realize that the mentee must learn on their own and they will most certainly learn the hard way in a number of areas. This is similar to the parent who has to endure watching their kids make mistakes.

There then must be a time when core values are established to provide the structure that is needed. Core values should be developed by both the mentor and the mentee. This should start with casual conversation and work its way toward a more formal approach which is put in writing and even signed by both parties depending on what you are trying to accomplish with the relationship. For example, if the mentee has an issue with boundaries, it will be crucial for the mentee to help in adopting the core values as well as signing a document with their commitment to abide by these core values. Don't forget that the mentor must also abide by the same core values.

Never be afraid to say it like it is. Truth is the one thing that people must hear. Of course, we have to have discretion as to  how we say things. We must give nuggets of truth along with the encouragement to overcome whatever the obstacle is. For example, I was asked to speak at Donovan State Prison in San Diego, California. I was initially asked to speak alongside Lalo Gunther, who was to share his story with the inmates. At the last minute, the prison denied access to Lalo due to his past conviction. I was not anticipating my being the primary speaker. What was I to say to the inmates? I showed Lalo's video, and the group was definitely touched. The room was quiet, and as the video ended, I stood, walked to the front of the room, and began to speak.

I began asking the inmates why they were in the position they were in. They began telling me why they were in prison. I stopped them. I asked them what initially led them to the lifestyle choices they had made. Most in the room said it was because they did not have a dad. I had many things I wanted to respond right then; however, I held my thoughts, waiting for the right moment. After about fifteen minutes had passed, I asked the group of inmates if they had kids of their own, to which they excitedly raised their hands proclaiming their fatherhood. In this group of at least fifty inmates, almost all of them had children. I then said firmly but quietly, "You complaint that you are here because you lacked a father, yet you now do to your kids exactly what you have faulted your fathers for!" You could have heard a pin drop in this room. The men sat silent, appearing dazed. I then told them, "Until you turn your hearts back to your children, you will continue in a vicious cycle of a chaotic life." I explained to them that they are consumed with their desires, and wants, and that life is not about them—it is about their kids, and what sacrifices they can make for their kids!

As I left, I was not sure how the men had taken what I said. A few weeks went by and I received a letter from one of the inmates writing on behalf of the group of men. He told me how hard it was to hear what I said; however, they had been reflecting on what I said, and he wanted to thank me for the boldness to confront them with truth.

I believe mentees are looking for truth! They do not want fluff, they want pure truth, and someone to walk alongside them to help them through their life of self-confrontation.

The next stage deals in transparency. For the mentor to attempt to get the mentee to open up without first opening up to the mentee is counterproductive. The more the mentor becomes transparent, the more the mentee will open up. The mentor must make sure they never act shocked when the mentee begins to disclose things to them. Often times a mentee will disclose something that really catches the mentor off guard. No matter what happens, the mentor must be very careful with their body language and response to whatever is divulged. For example, if the mentee tries to disclose something, and the mentor shows signs of being stunned, the mentee will shut down.

It is vital for you to allow the mentee to open up to you. The more they disclose things to you and see that you have not given up on them, the more it cements your relationship. I cannot begin to tell you the kinds of things I have had people share with me. From infidelity to deep, deep secrets, I have heard it all. The more you find people sharing these things with you the more it should compliment you that they are entrusting things to you.

For a mentoring relationship to be successful, there are certain things a mentee can do to make the mentoring connection optimal. This occurs, of course, when the mentee recognizes the need to be mentored.

The mentee has to want to be a partner in the mentoring connection. To that end, they prepare and do the appropriate "homework" for meetings with their mentor. They work to gain the skills, knowledge, and abilities to grow. They're flexible, listen to their mentor, and consider new options. They take initiative, seeking the mentor's advice when needed. And they focus on the goal, not getting lost in the process (if it isn't clear, they ask the mentor how the process leads to the goal).

The mentee has to know and be able to discuss their needs and objectives with their mentor. This means that he or she has to look inside themselves to identify areas that may need work and share them with the mentor.

The mentee must take responsibility for his or her career and goals. Although they have the benefit of the mentor's guidance, they are responsible for their own path. The mentor may guide the mentee on the path to earn a promotion, for instance, but it is the mentee who must earn it.

The mentee needs to be able to receive feedback and look at the situation from the mentor's perspective to gain a more objective viewpoint. One of the biggest values of the connection is the ability to have a more experienced person's viewpoint; sometimes when it is our own situation we are looking at, we cannot see the forest for the trees.

The mentee has to be willing to try new things, to consider different ways of "getting there from here."

The mentee has to periodically assess the progress of the relationship, letting the mentor know when priorities must be reset.

A good example of a solid mentor relationship can be evidenced by an individual I met years ago. Garry Gison is serving in the U.S. Army Reserves and works in the civilian world. Garry has been a faithful friend and describes his boss being his mentor. Garry describes what mentoring means to him:

Mentorship: An Equal Opportunity Employer

A lot of people identify mentoring as a temporary buddy system between adults and young people. Any other type of mentorship is labeled as a tutor, counselor or a teacher of an apprentice. Mentoring to me is comparable to a social worker or counselor, except that it is not a paid position. It is not a temporary position, nor is it something you can put on your resume. A mentor is someone who invests in another person's life and always looks out for that person's best interests. Mentoring demands a lot of a person's time, money and effort. This type of mentoring is not limited to young people alone. It can also be found in professional sport teams or at any work place. It can be in any environment with any person, no matter what age.

I am currently being mentored by Jose Silva, my boss in a medical supply store. Although our relationship is business related, whereas I am an employee and he an employer, mentorship does not stop here. Mentorship is a 24/7 indiscriminate and equal opportunity type employer. Anyone can be a mentor to anyone! Let me explain further.

My boss is my mentor. Jose Silva is part owner of a family-owned Triad Medical Supply store in the city of La Mesa, San Diego. He is an experienced business owner who has started and managed many corporations before managing a medical supply store. I started working for him in July of 2007. My job as an employee is to be a cashier, stock  person, salesman, and a deliverer of medical supplies to our clients outside our store. Jose is in charge of managing the store and his employees. He puts a lot of effort into teaching me a lot about selling items, customer relationships, management and leadership skills. Why? Jose sees me as a potential store manager because he sees the qualities I have as fitting well with his position. However, he realizes that my direction in life and my goals do not reflect the direction he wants me to be in. Does that stop him from teaching me the qualities of a store manager?

Although he knows that I will not be the one that takes over his store as a manager, Jose Silva still teaches me the qualities of leadership and management. Why? Jose saw that I needed some guidance in my life when it comes to school, relationships and life skills. He teaches me about time management, memory exercises to help me with memory and also tells me stories of how he dealt with his employees when he was a manager of other business companies. He leads by example, showing me how he wants me to be—not only a good employee, but also an example as a leader. He corrects me when I make mistakes and compliments me when I do the right things. Finally, he puts time and effort in me, allowing me to see that he actually cares about my outcome as a person. His efforts in mentoring me have caused me to become a more confident and able person who realizes that limitations in thought and ability don't start and end in the mind. In other words, just because you don't think you can, doesn't mean you can't.

There are several things I would like to point out to you as to why I identify him as a mentor. First, he leads by example. If he is teaching me how to be punctual when it comes to work, he demonstrates it by being an hour or two early before the store opens and before I come in to work. When I come in to work for him, he shakes my hand the very first thing in the order of business. By shaking my hand, he is telling me that he is always on time and that he will always be waiting for me and not me waiting on him.

Second, he always inquires as to the progress I'm making in my life. He is not doing it as a matter of a greeting or to make a conversation to pass the time. Instead, he asks me because he really wants to know! This is important because if you are mentoring someone and you want that person to see that your friendship with him is genuine, you have to make it genuine.

Third, he sees through my past flaws and recognizes that I am a person with potential. "Potential with what?" you may ask. He sees that I can not only be a potential manager but also can also become a better person of quality than the way I am currently. It is also because he knows me! He knows that I am a soldier in the United States Army. The skills and values I bring to the workplace directly reflect my membership in the Armed Forces. He knows also that my interest in life is in the medical field. I work for an ambulance company and am currently going to school to become a Physical Therapy Assistant at San Diego Mesa College. Having said that, you have to know the person whom you are mentoring so that you can see his or her potential and verbalize it to them so that they know they have potential. It makes the person feel special and recognized and not just an ordinary static person or client. You also are able to see a mentee's skills, quality and the direction in their life so that you can guide them to take advantage of their potentiality. Jose knows me well so he can guide me to become a better person in life. He sees my potential, and that is important.

Fourth, when there were times I needed some on-the-spot correction, he does not shy away from it whether I like it or not. You can't be a good mentor if one always wants to please the person and not correct him if he does wrong. There are times when I am helping out a customer that he has had to correct me on the spot because I was giving the customer wrong or misleading information about our services. There are other times when he has taken me over to the side and corrected me because I didn't follow procedure. He doesn't correct me to boss me around; he does it so that I will not hurt the business or that I don't make the same mistakes over and over again. This is why it is important to give on-the-spot correction.

If you know of someone who likes to binge drink everyday, you have to tell him to take responsibility for his life and not binge. If you don't tell him to correct his ways, then he will always have a potential for being tardy or absent from class. Furthermore, he can also become a drunk driver because alcohol impairs judgment. It doesn't matter if he knows he can't drink and drive. If his judgment is impaired, then he will not make intelligent or common sense decisions. Making timely and constructive corrections saves a mentee from possible errors they will regret.

Last but not least, he puts time and effort into mentoring me regardless if I don't always meet his standards or expectations. When I have made mistakes and he has had to correct me, he has done a follow-up. He makes sure that I don't make the same mistakes over and over by either re-teaching me the procedures, or he having me do some practicing to condition my mind, so that if I am presented with the same situation then I will not be making the same mistakes. This type of follow-up requires planning and patience, both of which take effort. In the same way, it takes time to meet with the person whom you are mentoring. It takes money to get there. It takes effort to teach and re-teach the person if he doesn't understand. It takes a great deal of creativity to solve his problems. It even takes an emotional toll if the person has a lot of issues. However, at the end, the result of your efforts will less likely come back void and without benefits to both you and that person. The amount of time and effort Jose has invested in my life has caused me to be more confident and skillful not only at the workplace but also in many aspects of my life. For Jose, his efforts have equally increased revenue for the store and have increased the number of customers coming into the store. Most important, his efforts may have given him the satisfaction that he can change lives in a positive manner.

Mentorship is an equal opportunity employer. Regardless of status, sex, age or religion, you can mentor anyone who needs mentorship in any environment. In my case, it happens to be in my job. It does take a great deal of time and effort to mentor someone. However, the outcome of your efforts as a mentor (if you so choose to be) will make your mentee and you become better persons.

CHAPTER 5

▼

A MENTOR'S POSITIONAL STRENGTH

"Positional strength" can be defined as the positioning of oneself to reach maximum effectiveness in influencing others. To have this positional strength requires open and honest introspection to discern your own strengths and weaknesses. We must be receptive to receiving criticism from others. We must think outside of the box, and it is critical that we have set in place foundational core values.

A quick way to lose all positional strength is to violate the trust and share confidential information your mentee has entrusted to you. Steve Gonzalez of the San Diego-based DreamWeavers shares an exercise with people in training to become mentors. He asks them to write their deepest darkest secret on a piece of paper and for them to fold it. After everyone writes something down, he begins to collect the slips of paper, assuring everyone he will not read them aloud. He then jokes that he knows many people in the audience probably wrote nothing on their piece of paper. He then gathers all the pieces of paper and says he has decided he will read some of them. Of course the audience begins to feel some anxiety due to their discomfort with their deepest, darkest secret being revealed to the entire room. He then says he will not read them, but wanted them to see how it feels to have shared a deep, dark secret and then have it shared.

When you ask your friends to pray for your mentee and you use that as a way to compromise the trust given to you by your mentee, it is unconscionable. This so clearly illustrates the point my friend was trying to make.

Possessing this positional strength gives the mentor a platform with the greatest possible position held which can be used as leverage to help lead their mentee. For example, if the mentor does not lead by example, they will lose their positional strength. Diminishing our positional strength as a mentor has serious consequences. Enabling your mentee to establish manipulative control over you will totally undermine your positional strength. It will also weaken your leadership character, rendering useless your ability to lead.

A mentee can compliment you as a form of manipulative control. The first step is to not draw any kind of self-worth from your mentee. Additionally, if you realize you have lost your positional strength, you must try and regain it. To do this you must establish core values that you hold yourself and your mentee accountable to. For example, the core values must be defined by both the mentor and the mentee together. What are the expectations within the mentor relationship? These can be used as your core values. For example, keeping your word, respecting confidentiality, and having mutual values that are important to both the mentor and mentee. You must be consistent. You must value your positional strength more so than you want to be accepted by your mentee.

Consider desired results and outcomes. Consider weaknesses within your leadership. Try to reinforce the set core values *intrinsically* rather then *extrinsically*. Intrinsic motivation comes from deeply held beliefs while extrinsic motivation is derived from externalities.

These externalities are basically this for that. Quid pro quo! For example, a parent telling their child for every "A" they receive on their report card, they will get fifty dollars. This may work in the short-term, but in the long run they will be motivated for the wrong reason and it will undermine the core values being taught to that individual.

Operational strength can be defined as the best possible position to accomplish set goals. Another strategy a mentor should use to gain positional and operational strength with their mentee is to help the mentee create a personal mission statement for their life. In the last chapter of this book, you will be led through the process of creating a personal mission statement for your life.

The mentor should share their personal mission statement as well. Establish core values within the relationship that support the personal mission statement that each of you has created.

Another crucial part of positional strength is understanding what it means to be an anchor for your mentee. Being an anchor lays the foundation for consistency and steadiness that will really set the tone for the mentee to grow. A good anchor mentor will build up the mentee so that even the mere mention of the mentors name brings remembrance of how much the mentor believed in the mentee, thus being that anchor of support for the mentee.

This positional strength holds very true for leaders within organizations. When I was young, I recall hearing parents blame each other for having to tell their child 'no'. For example, a child would ask their parent to take them somewhere, and instead of their mother saying she would rather they not go, she would say, "No, you know how your dad is, he will not let you." A mother would have been in a better position to simply say that she and their dad did not think it was a good idea. Because the mother did not, her response would allow the child to pit one parent against the other as a form of manipulation to get their own way.

In the same way, sometimes a manager in an organization will blame the company for policies and rules instead of understanding that the manager and employees really are "The Company." A manager has much stronger positional strength when the manager uses terms such as, "We as a company must ensure that …" instead of, "The Company says that we …" or, "You know how the company is …"

Sometimes leaders do not want to be the "bad guy." It seems much easier at times to blame an organization for things instead of encouraging everyone to stick together when particular dilemmas occur. Taking responsibility can be modeled for employees so that they all function as a large, integrated team.

A Mentor Mindset

A mentor must have a mindset that develops over time. This mindset always seeks opportunities to develop those around us. Anytime we meet someone, we are looking for ways to plant seeds, encourage and motivate the person to doing greater things in their lives.

Perhaps one of the steadiest individuals I have ever met who never compromises his positional strength is Agustin Pena. Agustin recently lost his fourteen year-old brother in August 2007. I have never seen an individual endure the most heart-wrenching experience, yet serve others all the while he has endured the pain. Agustin is my right-hand man, and I cannot believe the level of maturity he possesses. I love Agustin with all of my heart and am awed at his words he will share.

The Agustin Pena Story
In Loving Memory of Javier Quiroz

In light of recent events in my life I am reflecting on the delicacy of life. As you will read, I have recently experienced a tremendous loss in my family, and I would like to encourage everyone to think twice about their lives in hopes that they do not take things for granted and live with the notion that tomorrow is promised. This philosophy is the most selfish that one could live by, for all

In Loving Memory
Javier Quiroz
4/15/93 - 8/27/07

we know tomorrow may never come so I ask that we all take advantage of today and impact someone in a positive way.

"Father of mine tell me where have you been, you know I just closed my eyes my whole world disappeared," are the beginning lyrics of a song called "Father of Mine." I have kept these lyrics in the back of my mind and in the deepest areas of my heart for years. There's nothing the world can offer that will ever hurt us more than the void an absent father leaves behind, or at least that was my belief until August 2007, but that's a story of its own. Even more unfortunate is the fact that this hurt *does* last for a very long time. Many will not admit it due to a fear of ridicule or mockery, but the pain one feels is real. It resides in us, and out of it will come many emotions, insecurities, and false ideations about oneself. Little did I know that the absence of the love only a father could give to his child was going to be the root of many obstacles during my life.

All of us have a biological father; otherwise, we wouldn't be here today. What I lacked in my life was a dad, a person I could admire and someone to teach me about life's struggles and be there to help me up when I fell. But I didn't have that because my father walked out of my life when I was three years old. Now, at age twenty-two, I have had very minimal contact with him, contact that I could no longer continue due to his treatment of my mother several years ago. I do not hold any resentment or have anger towards him, although the profound scars serve as a memory and today as motivation for me to help others in similar struggles.

Growing up, I heard about the great time that my friends had with their dads over the weekend. How much fun it would have been to have someone who's never too tired to play, never too tired to help you with homework, or even just to talk. At times I even thought *they* were the odd ones; I thought it was normal for kids to live in single-parent homes, or move back and forth between their mom's house and their grandparents' house. At the time I didn't think much of it, figuring that one day I would meet my dad and we would become a family once again.

To my surprise, holidays came and went without a call or a single word from him. It was at these moments that I could empathize with the kids whose dads couldn't go to their Baseball game, or Soccer practice. I knew what they felt, but I felt like that all the time.

Initially, I had lots of hope for having a relationship with my dad, but as the disappointments continued, my hope started to dissipate like a wave as it approaches the shore. It was at this point that I begin to wonder if he even remembered me, or if he thought about me. You can't help but question your own existence on this planet.

Why was I born if all I'm here for is to suffer? Why don't I have a dad? Is there something wrong with me? What if it's just me? Am I weak for feeling like this? These were some of the most frequent recurring thoughts in my head at the time. As much as I wanted to make sense of it all, I was just too overwhelmed by feelings of loneliness and despair. I felt like crying out to the world for help, but I didn't; instead, I kept it all bottled in. The multitude of emotions that I felt were at times too much to handle, but as bad as it became I could not confide in anyone to express how I truly felt. I had nobody to relate to, nobody that could understand. For years I would feel like this, some days more than others. But with time I slowly started to forget about it and became inured to my situation. I gradually became accustomed to the idea that I wasn't meant to have a father in my life. Although this did complicate things for me, and still does sometimes, I knew I had to move on with life or at least try to.

Just as I thought that my life could not become more compli-
cated and more bombarded with emotions, August 27, 2007
arrived. That day will be forever engraved in both my mind and in
my heart.

I received a call late Sunday night on August 26, a phone call that
placed me in such a turmoil that I always knew existed, but never
expected to experience. My mom was on the other end of the line
screaming, and I could barely understand what she was saying, let
alone identify who was saying it. "Agustin! Agustin! Javy was shot!
He's not moving, he was shot!" Javier was my fourteen year old
brother.

"What! What happened? Why? Who? Where?" I frantically
replied to the panicky yelling on the other end of the line. Shortly
after this heart-wrenching phone call, I hung up and lay in bed for a
while. I thought to myself, "Wait a minute, this can't happen to us.
He's gonna come through and we're gonna take him home and
everything will go back to normal." Although I attempted to ratio-
nalize the severity of that night's events, I was still very concerned
over the fact that my brother wasn't moving when my mother
found him next to a near-by street light. After a few minutes I
decided to drive over to the hospital. Then I began to cry. I cried
out of worry that he wouldn't make it and I would lose my one and
only brother. On the way to the hospital I called Kevin LaChapelle
and advised him of what was going on, he also began to cry. It was
near midnight when I was driving to the hospital and I arrived
shortly after 12:00 AM. I told Kevin I would call him again as soon
as I received some information on my brother's status. I went
directly to the waiting area and asked to see my family. I was
informed that no one was allowed to proceed into the back room

because it was already full of people. I was irritated, but continued to keep my composure because I did not want to be escorted off of the property. Although I was unable to see my family in the rear waiting area, I called my mom to let her know that I had arrived and was waiting outside. While waiting, I had been talking to my girlfriend Liz, trying to explain to her what happened, at least what I knew at the moment about what happened. Then I received a call on the other line from a blocked number so I automatically knew that it was my mom calling from inside the hospital. I asked Liz to wait on the line while I got some news about my brother's condition. In the most heart-broken sobbing voice, my mother said, "He's dead, he's dead … They couldn't save him." I was left speechless for a few moments. I felt like someone had punched me right in the chest, and I could not breathe. "No no no, please no!" I kept pleading to my mom as if she could somehow change the circumstances. My brother was gone, he was dead … All of a sudden I was plagued once again with so many thoughts and emotions because my world, my reality, had been torn to pieces as if an emotional cyclone had come through and wreaked havoc on everything I knew and loved. I switched lines and repeated the news to Liz. Her response was very similar to mine. I explained to her that I could not speak at the moment; I had to go inside to be with my family. She understood, so we ended our phone call shortly after. As I entered the hospital waiting room, my cousins came out with open arms, sobbing, repeating my mom's words, "He's gone man, Javy's gone." I received them with open arms as well, and the three of us stood together sobbing for a few moments in the middle of the hallway.

My family and I spent about four hours at the hospital that night, mostly because the shock hadn't worn off yet, and we were calling relatives and neighbors to make them aware of this tragedy. After we all left the hospital, it felt as though I had left something behind. While I was taking my mom home, I kept feeling as if I had forgotten something, and deep down I knew that although I *was* in fact leaving someone, it was not due to my forgetting him. I had originally planned to leave my mom at her apartment and go home to get some rest, because it was already after four in the morning. I couldn't resist; I had to go down to the area where my brother took his final steps and muttered his last words.

Everything happened on 52nd Street near a local park, just a block away from 51st, the street on which my mom currently lives. While walking to where neighbors had set up a memorial for Javier, I was still in complete disbelief. I had just finished speaking to him three hours prior to his death and now I knew I'd never speak to him again. Shortly after arriving, I was touched by the immediate response of the entire community. There had to have been nearly fifty people underneath the light pole, which is a lot considering it's nearly 5:00 AM. I couldn't help but cry some more, as the dark realization sank in when I saw candles and pictures of him being placed next to the light pole.

I remained there for another hour until I finally decided that I needed to get some sleep. It seemed like the longest day of my life. Even then I only slept for only an hour or two, then I went back to my mom's apartment to see how she had been doing. I was so consumed with the loss of my brother that I had not yet realized I was about to embark on the longest week of my life, making arrangements for the cemetery, mortuary, burial and starting my own sixteen-unit fall semester at San Diego State University the next day.

It was difficult to envision the light at the end of the tunnel during those early stages of my brother's passing. People tell me that death is a natural part of life, with which I fully agree—but murder isn't. Murder is completely unnatural. Nobody's brother, son, daughter niece or nephew should be brutally taken away from them. Unfortunately it does happen. It happens so frequently that it becomes all too common in some parts of the world, which is why now, more than ever, the world needs leaders who work for good! Leaders who can stand up to protect the weak in their times of need. These leaders, or mentors, can, and usually are, the deciding factor in a person's life. I have had the opportunity to observe first-hand the powerful influence that one can have over others. The friendship that a mentor can offer an individual who sees no hope for his/her future is what we call a glimmer of hope. That glimmer of hope helps one realize one's potential in life and ultimately begins to empower individuals to strive. As mentors we never ask for anything in return except for one thing: That the individuals we mentor pass on the teachings and keep the cycle alive, because someone somewhere is yearning for a purpose.

Though it is hard enough to mentor someone when life appears to be playing out in your favor, it is all the more difficult to guide someone when enduring tough times. Since my brother's passing, I have battled with bitterness and anger toward myself and the world. There were many times I felt like giving up and throwing away everything I've worked for. But I always go back to the knowledge that I would be letting everyone around me down. I am aware that there are a lot of people counting on me to succeed, and I know that if I give up on life right now, it would affect a lot of people indirectly and many more directly. Instead, I try to let my brother's memory be my fuel everyday. That's the way it was before he passed on. I tried to create a reality for him that was once foreign to me. The reality that he could also go to college to further his education. Unfortunately, that will never be his reality, he was destined for something else. If not my brother's life, I at least want to make this someone else's reality. Whether it be a neighbor that I normally see, or someone I've never even spoken a word to. I would like everyone to know that the opportunities are there, but one just needs to be persistent and aim for the stars. We all have the capabilities to accomplish great things, the same objective is not everybody's focus but we each have a certain goal we would like to see all the way through. The question is not what your goal or purpose is, but what are you doing *now* to accomplish it. I work with juvenile detainees, and I hear all the time that they would like to go to college once they are released. Weeks later they wind up back in there for a simple violation. We need to understand that achieving goals will not happen on their own. To say, "I would like to go to college," is not the same as, "I am going to college." Half of what it takes to reach a goal is setting sub-goals, smaller goals that help you better arrive to your larger goal. Small things in life that assist you in progressing instead of hindering you, so you digress. The second portion is our will. How much do we want to accomplish this goal? If this goal isn't a priority in our lives, I can tell you for sure that we will always stray from it and before you know it, you're saying "someday I would *like* to do this …" Which is why it's also important that we want to reach this goal, not only reach it but reach it for the right reasons.

Here is when mentors come into play. Their role is essential in helping find that goal, setting up a plan to reach it, and assisting along the way. One aspect of mentoring that most people aren't aware of is that it can be a "two-way street." The mentor is just as capable of learning from the relationship as the individual he/she is mentoring. Another key to a successful mentoring relationship is one's life experiences. These valuable pearls of wisdom may be considered common sense to some people, but to others they may be a perspective they've never seen before. People may sometimes look at you like you are out of this world or like you're speaking a foreign language. But I've noticed more often than not, people want to hear these things. It's very rare that someone will turn away from you, rejecting any help; as a matter of fact, I don't remember that ever happening. Therefore, one must never assume that everyone knows these things. As contradictory as it sounds, common sense is relative.

Life, such a small word and yet it has the most meaning to different people. Life is one of the most difficult endeavors that anyone will experience because life encompasses school, work, family, friends love, etc. There will never be a point at which one will suffer no more; on the contrary, life is almost synonymous with suffering. Setting aside the negative connotation of suffering, suffering allows one to grow and learn. Although one undergoes some painful experiences in life, those experiences can contribute to the personal growth and development of the individual. For example, I was always conscious that I would try and turn every negative event into some learning experience. The absence of a father figure, choices I made during high school that I regret, and now my brother's passing. It's always best if we attempt to find purpose in even the worst of circumstances because in the end we walk away with something subjective. We walk away with a brand new experience that nobody else has been through. Although some people are able to understand one's situation, they will never fully comprehend it. We are the only individuals who experience these events and live them day by day; therefore, we are the only ones who walk away with the wisdom from that situation or event.

In my opinion, the most difficult part of life is not the experience in and of itself, but applying the lesson you have learned from it. At first glance this opinion may seem counter-intuitive, but think about it a little further, and you will also conclude the same. Life can throw obstacles at us, many of which we can overcome. In most cases, its necessary for us to overcome them; otherwise, we will no longer be able to continue in a productive life. But while overcoming these obstacles, most people will forget about the lessons learned. Experiences are nothing without the lessons, just as wisdom is merely knowledge without its application. What good is it if we experience issues in which we are broken down to our most vulnerable selves, if we don't learn something from our situation? The same is true with the lessons. What good is experiencing tough circumstances if the lessons we learn are stored away in our memories and are never acted upon? The answer to both questions is that it is not good at all. As a matter of fact the experience becomes a waste of time. If the kids who returned to the juvenile correction facility applied what they learned while in jail, they would not have returned. Again, people often cannot do this by themselves, which leads me once more to the mentor. This is what I referred to as the mentor being the deciding factor in one's life. Leadership is what most individuals lack during their lives, and leadership is exactly what a mentor can provide. It would be unfair for me to point the finger at everyone and claim that it's their own fault, when in fact I am aware that sometimes we can't do it on our own. Of the cases I have encountered, a lot, maybe even most, have yearned for that leadership and purpose in life. It's human nature to want to belong; we all want to claim that we belong to something.

No matter how old, regardless of economical status, race, or ethnicity, everyone yearns for a purpose in this brief endeavor we call life. Despite the fact that life will often times be difficult for us, keep in mind that someone, somewhere, is praying for guidance. Someone, in a much worse scenario than ours, is trying to stay positive in hopes that someone, will be able to help set them on a good path.

I dedicate my words and all of the accomplishments that I achieve in my life to my little brother Javier Quiroz. You will always be missed and never forgotten. I love you, and wherever you are I hope that one day we will see each other again.—Agustin Peña

Walking the Talk

One of the greatest attributes of Agustin Pena is the fact that he walks the talk. He is an example of everything he teaches to his mentees. Being an example cannot be understated and is a key in mentoring others.

There have been many times when I have seen how a poor example, or someone who talks the talk but clearly does not walk the walk can undermine the entire mentoring process. For example, I was sent to the LAPD's D.A.R.E. (Drug Awareness Resistance Education) Academy. It was a very interesting experience. I met two other officers at this academy, one of whom I still keep in touch. His name is Ramon Godoy. The first night of class, police officers from all over the United States and even some other countries arrived for this training. The first thing I noticed was that the majority of officers were drinking alcohol excessively, and here we were at a D.A.R.E. Academy where we would learn to teach the youth the dangers of alcohol and drugs.

Almost instantly, Ramon, Fabian, and I all seemed to catch each others' eyes. I recall the three of us sitting separately, but looking around and watching what was happening at a mixer event designed to help us all get to know one another. After a short time, Ramon made his way over to me, and we introduced ourselves to each other. It was not long before Fabian joined us. The three of us immediately had a strong bond, and we talked about our mutual interests in helping communities. We would soon learn that all three of us had personal relationships with God.

Throughout the training, each night the same thing would happen over and over again. The officers would get drunk and act foolish. The next day they would sit in a classroom being lectured on the negatives associated with alcohol and drugs, which we must instill in our future students. This was so ironic.

For our final presentation, we had to give a lecture as if it were to young people on the dangers of alcohol and drugs. My presentation was much different than anyone might have guessed. Instead of speaking to the officers as if they were young people as we were instructed, I addressed the police officers as if they were my D.A.R.E. officer, and as if I were their student. I began the presentation by talking about how much of an impact my D.A.R.E officer had on me, and that I looked up to and respected him so much. I talked about the fact that he was the inspiration that I needed to resist alcohol and drugs and that I wanted to be somebody in life and be a role model just like my D.A.R.E. officer.

The closing of my presentation took a major turn. I told a story about right after graduating from the D.A.R.E. program at my school. My parents wanted to treat me to dinner to congratulate me. We went to a local pizzeria. During dinner I was telling my parents how great my D.A.R.E. Officer was, and how much I looked up to him. And then, I got excited because I saw that very D.A.R.E. officer eating dinner with his friends at the same pizzeria. I took my parents over to meet the officer. As we approached, we could hear how boisterous he and his friends were, and I could see that my hero, my role model, was drinking the very alcohol that he had said was dangerous for me. The look on his face was one that I would never forget. He did not say anything, for he knew the hypocrisy of his lessons at school, which he did not follow himself.

You could hear a pin drop in this classroom full of police officers. The looks started off as sincere reflections of all of the partying these officers had done at night while learning about the dangers of alcohol and drugs during the day. That soon changed as they began to resent my calling attention to this, and then many of them shrugged it off as if to say, "Can you believe this guy, who does he think he is?" Some officers approached me later, acknowledging that they needed to practice what they preached. I hoped they would remember that story. The bottom-line, if you are going to mentor someone, is that you had better practice what you preach, or you will be more of a hindrance than a help to the people you mentor.

CHAPTER 6

▼

EXPERIENTIAL
MENTORING

For many years I would be frustrated by the many experiences I had in my life. From the poor relationship I had with my father to my difficulties in school. There have been many times that my weaknesses in life have been overwhelming. Why did I have to go through the things I went through? Why did I have to have Attention Deficit Hyperactive Disorder (ADHD)? Why am I such a nonconformist?

I would later learn that all of these issues in my life would give me the strength to understand others and the ability to lead. One of the greatest tools I have is the fact that those around me continually see me deal with my own struggles, and they quickly recognize that they are not alone in their despair. If you are mentoring others with the mindset that your life is all together and you are just there for this poor lost soul, your motives are not only in question, but your arrogant attitude will undermine everything good you try to do for your mentee.

None of us can claim perfection. None of us can claim we have no issues in our own life. For a mentee to open up to their mentor, usually the mentor must first open up and share the challenges they face in their own life. Make sure you do not fall into the trap of one-upping your mentee. For example, many mentors fall into talking about who had a worse life, and the mentee tells stories, and the mentor tells even greater stories, etc. This is very counter-productive. We can never fully understand what others have been through, and when we act as though we know, we are hindering the experiential learning process both the mentor and mentee must go through.

I now have learned not to regret my past experiences, but rather embrace them, for they have made me who I am today. In other words, had I not experienced a poor relationship with my father, I would never have had the passion to be there for others as I do today.

I recall men who saw something in me and chose to mentor me. The first mentor I encountered in my life was an elderly neighbor. His name was Mr. Sylvester. I would see him watering his lawn, and he would very specifically get my attention by waving to me and ask how I was doing. He would always make a comment about how special I was. He caught my attention, that is for sure.

Mr. Sylvester never told me he was there to help me or anything like that. He just began to develop a relationship with me that was very subtle. Before I knew it, we were very close. He always would point out my strengths. He said very little about my weaknesses. Occasionally, he would see negative behavior in me, and he would gently make a comment. For example, if he saw me arguing with my mom, he would later tell me how much he missed his mother and how he wished he had treated her better. He methodically planned and calculated every action and mostly used his experiences in life to meet me on common ground.

Mr. Sylvester had a wife who was very sick. He would be careful not to get frustrated with her when I would be at their house. I now can look back and see that he was modeling the love that a man should have for his wife. At the time, I did not notice those things, but I surely do now.

Mr. Sylvester helped me plan my life. He knew that he could not force me to do anything, so he just made comments and allowed me to question him when it was something that jumped out at me.

I remember thinking to myself, "I wonder what this guy sees in me." Mr. Sylvester thought I was the greatest, and he was not afraid to tell me that frequently. He was very wise in his leading me.

Mr. Sylvester probably had the most profound impact on me during my teen years. He was so sensitive to what I might be dealing with. When I began to experience acne, he showed me how to clean my face with Aloe Vera, which cleared my face up in no time. He wanted the best for me, and wanted to be a part of making me the best; I could feel it. Likewise, I energized Mr. Sylvester and his wife. All of the energy I brought with me showered them with excitement.

When I disappointed Mr. Sylvester, he did not have to say anything, as I knew I had not listened to him, and I would suffer the consequence for it. He never would tell me, "I told you so." He would just smile and tell me it was part of growing up and learning the hard way.

Another mentor I had when I joined the police department was my lieutenant. The first watch commander I had was Chuck Donovan. This guy was something else. He was the dad I never had. Chuck's personality was incredible. First, he was a strong man. This man did not take anything off of anyone. He was not that large of a man, yet rarely did anyone on the street question his phenomenal command presence. I would define his command presence as a demeanor composed of a confident, but calm, assertive approach to everything. This calm, assertive approach is what many parents need to master in raising their teenagers. Much credibility is lost when people lash out in an emotional rant, causing a lot of damage to a relationship. Chuck had that 'tough love' approach in which his words were powerful because they were strategically said to discipline you, but to also follow up with a nurturing love. He also had a gentle, caring side to his personality. He had a good sense of humor. His greatest attribute was that he genuinely cared about others and would share little bits of wisdom here and there.

I remember at first not knowing what to make of him. He would playfully grab me throwing me against the wall when I would walk by at the police station. He was rough and tough. He would toss you across the room in a playful manner, which was full of affection. He let you know when you did something wrong, and praised you when you did something right. He was known as the protector. If you ever were out there in a mess and needed some strong-man power, he was the lieutenant you wanted on your side. I remember a few times he would show up on a radio call, and he would stand by us as if we were his sons.

Chuck would encourage me to stand up for what I believed in. He had a deep faith in God. He and I had a lot in common in that we were both raised Catholic. We differed in our beliefs. He was like my mom who was very into the Catholic tradition, while I was more into having a personal relationship with God rather than the Church thing or the tradition. Our differences never came between us. There was a mutual trust and respect. Chuck was somewhat of a nonconformist himself, to which I could relate well.

Another mentor for me was Joe Meeker who was a weight-training coach at one of the high schools that catered to the at-risk student population. He and I were introduced by the principal, who felt we would work well together in helping the gang members change. Joe was very similar to Chuck—a strong man who was known as a protector who could not be fooled by anyone. On the other hand, he also had that gentle, loving side. Not only was I drawn to him, but also countless at-risk students were as well. He was that dad role model so many longed for.

Joe also saw the good in me and drew out as much as he could. He would share with me what talent he could see and would advise me how to expand upon it. Joe would tell me if I was wrong. He was also a bit of a nonconformist. It is interesting to me that the guys whom God put in my life had a lot in common with me. They were both nurturing and disciplining influences in my life.

Lastly, a man that God put in my life to show me the example I needed to see was Tom Godley. When I served on an elected school board, Tom was our superintendent. Tom was an incredible man. He was principally centered in his decision making and leadership. He was the most consistent and steady person I had ever known. He was not a tough guy; he was a sensible  guy. He would share so much wisdom with me that I think I learned and grew from him more than anyone ever in my life. Tom also taught ethics at the university level.

The interesting part of this relationship was that I was the president of the school board, while Tom worked for us. Tom always respected my role, yet he knew of my inexperience and was so patient in guiding me to try to do the best I could. Tom also had a strong faith in God, which I could tell was his whole foundation in life. I admired that so much and will never forget the impact he had on my life.

The experiences we encounter in life are what lead us to growth and understanding. A great example of this truth comes from two individuals who have been very near and dear to my heart. Mario and his wife Karina are incredible individuals. They have been through so much, yet they know it is the rough experiences that they have endured that make them effective mentors for others. Here is their story:

The Mario and Karina Torres' Story

Certain events in my life come to mind, and those very things would help me relate to my best friend, who would later be my wife. I was raised in a neighborhood where "the gang life" was an everyday struggle, mostly because of the core gang sub-culture in my family. That brought a huge influence which was starting to have draw me into the sub-culture.

My role models during my early teens were older family members who did not make wise decisions. They were tattooed and unfortunately abused alcohol and drug substances. Sadly, these relatives, who were a huge influence during my early teens, made wrong choices in life. I know for a fact that they now regret their choices and wish they could turn back the clock to the time in which they could have made the right choice. This wish brings to mind their telling me to learn from their mistakes.

Because the image of toughness was all around me, it was my perspective of what I wanted to be during my early teens. I felt it gave me respect from my peers in school; however, now that I really think about it, it was most likely fear rather than respect. I hung out with friends who also seemed to be drawn into the gang culture.

I remember a situation that occurred in my early teens, when the police took a picture of me because of an incident that happened. A friend of mine assaulted someone, and the police believed it was gang related. I happened to be there. Already at that young age, I was being documented and labeled as a trouble-maker.

I went through many other situations and, due to my immaturity, faced many difficult circumstances. I ran away from home at the age of sixteen. I moved in with my uncle, and during the time I was living with him, his house was raided by law enforcement officers. I was at the learning center when the raid took place. My uncle was sentenced to seven years in prison. Even though he was one of my role models, I surely did not want to ever end up in prison.

Educationally, I did poorly during my elementary, middle and high school years. My first time for being suspended was in elementary school. Disciplinary issues were common for me through my middle and high school years as well. When I was in middle school, I remember kicking a flour baby in our parenting class. I was always trying to be the center of attention by making my peers laugh. I was placed in a program called R.S.P. I am not sure what the acronym stood for; however, others kids would tease me saying it stood for "Real Stupid People."

During the beginning of my sophomore year, I was expelled from my German class because my teacher was tired of my always distracting my colleagues from whatever he was teaching. My counselor placed me in a Mariachi music class where I did not want to be. At first, Mr. Tinoco, the Mariachi music instructor, happened to be in his first year of teaching at my high school. Because he was a rookie, it gave me an advantage to push the limit. Every time he wrote a referral for me to be sent to the principal's office, he would leave his copy attached. That gave me the opportunity to take an hour's break from school.

A person who mentored me during the most critical period of my life was that very same high school instructor, Mr. Tinoco. He gave me the opportunity that many other instructors did not. He did not succeed in changing my behavior then and there; however, he worked little by little in teaching me, not only music, but discipline. He taught me a different lifestyle, one other than gangs. He also taught me Mariachi.

Mr. Tinoco gave me the opportunity of being a member of his performing group, even though my citizenship grades were poor. The group performed at weddings, birthday parties, and open concerts. He kept us involved in the community by performing. This resulted in my staying away from negative influences. Since most performances were on the weekends, I could hardly see or hang out with the friends who were bad influences on me. After school I would stay and practice everyday for about two hours. Academically, I had to pick up my grades in order to be able to perform. Playing music motivated me. That is one item of advice I would give: Find what motivates your mentee and use that as a key for helping the mentee achieve his or her goals.

I managed to graduate from high school with my class in the year 2004, with a grade point average of 1.95. That was the biggest accomplishment for my life. I was the first person in my family to graduate from high school. I set many goals for myself and decided to continue my education. One of my goals was to major in Criminal Justice.

The summer of my high school graduation; the Mariachi group and I flew to Albuquerque, New Mexico, where we won second place in the Mariachi Spectacular Showcase. I then flew to Guadalajara, Mexico, for a huge Mariachi festival. I saw life a bit differently now that I was out of a bubble called the "neighborhood."

I was given the opportunity to teach for three years during the Mariachi conferences provided by the Sweetwater High School District. Immediately after I returned from Guadalajara, I started college. I obtained an Associate of Science degree in Criminal Justice and am currently working on my Bachelor's program. During the first year of my Associate's degree, I maintained a 4.0 G.P.A. I paid some tuition with money that I earned playing music on the weekends.

My music instructor warned me about certain situations that I might see in the music industry. He warned me that musicians and even clients might offer me illegal substances; because of the music, drug dealers might even hire the band for their parties. Of course, I witnessed many things; however, it wasn't until I was playing professionally that my eyes were really opened.

During the New Mexico and Guadalajara conferences, instructors at the conference would get drunk every night. I myself would drink as well. I would see great musicians with immense talent using illegal substances. Musicians for whom I had a high regard disappointed me when I saw them abusing drugs.

Many people have encouraged me to pursue a law enforcement career. A very good friend of mine, Mary Leon, who is an incredible individual, has taught me a variety of things. She herself was in law enforcement for approximately ten years and is someone who I look up to for her many accomplishments, most importantly her ethical example and her excellence in teaching. She is one of my college instructors. It's incredible how much mentors have impacted me and helped me mature. It changed my whole perspective on life and has allowed me to recognize that I am on the way to accomplishing my goal of one day being a member of law enforcement.

When I started dating my girlfriend, I think that was one of the best things that ever happened to me. She came to my life when I felt alone, even though I knew God was always there with me. On October 4, 2005, I heard my mother talking about being upset because she did not have enough money to pay bills. I went over to the living room, and we argued. I honestly believed what I was saying was justified. She suddenly became outraged, telling me to go to my room. I defiantly said, "No, I'm not a little kid who needs to be told what to do." She told me to shut up, which I did. I knew what my mother was capable of and kept in mind how she hit me when I was a child, so I did just as she said, even though I was in my late teens. I shut up. I know what I did was wrong by ignoring her when she was yelling for me to go to my room. She then told me to grab all of my things and leave. I left, but the first thing I grabbed was my Trajes de Charro, Mariachi outfits, and my guitar, because I knew having these would help me economically.

I heard my father coming to my room. I thought that he was going to defend me and tell me not to leave; however, he came in and said, "Your mother doesn't want you here, and I'm sorry but you have to leave." I honestly do not believe I said anything wrong, although I do acknowledge that I was wrong to ignore my mother's orders by not going to my room. I never thought she would kick me out. I remember asking myself, what have I done wrong? I had turned my life completely around, had stopped making poor choices in life, and was going to school. I paid my tuition with the money I made playing music on the weekends; my parents knew I did not have the means to pay rent. My father opened up to me for the first time the day my mother kicked me out. He told me that he knew how it felt to be kicked out of your own home, because when he was young his mother told him to leave too.

The only difference was that he thought he never had a future, coming in and out of the California Youth Authority, and involved in drugs and gangs. He said that I was different, that I had a future, and that he was very proud of me. That was the first time I ever saw my father cry. He gave me his pastor's phone number, since he had no money to give me that day, but he told me as soon as I found a place to live, to call him and he would help me in any way he could.

I moved to an apartment with my sister's fiancé. Three days later I went out with some friends and the girl whom I plan to spend the rest of my life with was there. She and I ended up talking, and I remember her telling me that she liked my personality. I told her right back, "I love your personality too." Something about her had grabbed my attention. I asked her out, just like that, not really knowing her at all. I think we had only seen each other maybe ten times prior to that. She said yes and that she had something to tell me.

She told me that she had been dating her high school instructor, Mr. Hernandez, who was the Mariachi instructor at Sweetwater High School. I told her I had no problem with that. While we were getting to know each other, I questioned her more about that "relationship" with her teacher. I asked her how long they had dated, and she said it had been for some time. She said that several times she tried to end the relationship but for some reason Mr. Hernandez knew how to get her to stay. No one really knew about my dating her for almost a week.

When Mr. Hernandez found out about us dating, he changed his behavior towards her completely. He would call her every night telling her that "she had no feelings," and ask her "How could you do that to me, knowing that I love you?" He asked her if being with me had any meaning to her. He mentioned that if she left him, nothing would have meaning and that his purpose in teaching would be lost. He would tell her that he would leave teaching if she left him. He met with her one afternoon when we had been dating for about three days, and convinced her to end our relationship. She called me that day crying, saying that she was really confused. It was hard to believe how much control he had over her. When I learned more about this incident, I knew that what she thought to be a relationship with her instructor was actually a situation that left her a victim of Mr. Hernandez, and I was the first to find out about this.

This relationship began with his calling her almost every day to see what she thought about rehearsal. At first, she didn't feel comfortable with his calls. He would tell her that she was very talented; she was one of the best violinists he had ever taught. She said that he always put her up as an example in class. She said he made her feel very special and brought her self-esteem up. He then started grooming her by telling her little things, such as that she was very beautiful, she looked very pretty that day, and that he liked how her outfit looked on her. She liked those comments, just like any other teenage girl would. She knew he liked her since he would tell her that he wished she was older so that they could date. They would spend hours on the phone talking about many things until the conversations started changing, little by little. He would talk about sexual subjects, like masturbation, and told her that he masturbates more than most men do. They did talk about having sexual intercourse, but not until she was of legal age. One day he invited her to his house to watch a movie and gave her an mixed alcoholic drink.

They started kissing and ended up having their first sexual encounter. That afternoon when he took her home, he told her that no one must find out about what had just happened. She said she felt bad because instead of his making her feel special, he was more focused on her not telling anybody about what had occurred. While they dated, she started noticing a change in him. He wasn't as interested in her, and he would make her feel that she was worthless. There were times when he actually urinated on her like a dog marking his territory. She also suspected that he was cheating on her with other members of the Mariachi group she was in, who were also minors. When she confronted him, he denied it. She said that he was very persuasive and knew exactly how to manipulate her. She tried many times to end the relationship but he knew exactly how to convince her to stay. She told me she would cry at nights, asking God to help her, that she didn't want to be in that relationship.

I know Carlos Hernandez; he bought alcohol for me and some friends when I was in high school. I remember going to Tijuana with him and some friends, drinking and listening to Mariachi bands. I always saw him with one of his female students, Genie, who turned out to be one of his many victims.

While my wife and I were dating, he called her while drunk, crying and asking her why she left him. He would tell her that her relationship with me wasn't going to last because she wasn't being honest with me. He told her that when I found out about their encounters, I would leave her. Little did he know that I already knew everything. It took me about eight months to help her realize that she had been victimized. I showed her different news articles and cases similar to hers, but she would still feel guilty and blamed herself for what had happened. One day she told me she wouldn't want her little sister to go through the same situation as she did. She also asked me, "Do you think I will ever talk about this and report this to authorities?" I told her, "Yes." The next day I told Kevin LaChapelle, my Victimology instructor, about the situation. He advised me to take her to the Police Department and file a report. I did just that on May 31, 2006. When I took my girlfriend to the National City Police Department, an officer told us that depending where Mr. Hernandez lived, that particular police agency would have to file the report. We weren't sure if he lived in the San Diego or in the National City jurisdiction, since he lived off of the 54 freeway, near Woodman. I told the Officer that he worked at Sweetwater High School, that many of the incidents occurred on school premises, and that was within the National City jurisdiction. He said that if Mr. Hernandez lived in San Diego, the San Diego Police should take the report. I then called SDPD, and they told me that if Mr. Hernandez was an instructor at Sweetwater High, NCPD should file the report. We could not believe how they were tossing the case back and forth. It was as if neither agency wanted to deal with it. That was when I decided to go to Channel Ten News. We made an appointment with Marti Emerald, their Investigative Reporter, on Thursday, June 1st, 2006.

When the news video taped my girlfriend's statement, they called San Diego Police and notified them that they had the statement on video. The police department was advised that if they didn't take action, the video would be aired, notifying the public that authorities did not investigate the case. The police then obtained a search warrant. Mr. Hernandez was then arrested at Sweetwater High School on June 6, 2006, with thirty-two counts. He pled not guilty to the charges. However, a video with Genie was found in his bedroom, along with a recorded phone call. Also, other victims came forward and helped the prosecution. The prosecutor plea-bargained, agreeing to drop some charges if he pled guilty to others to spare the victims of a trial. He did and was charged with five counts. He was sentenced, on May 29, 2007, to six months in a work furlough program with five years probation. Mr. Hernandez will also have to register as a sex offender for life. Of course he also lost his teaching position and he will never be able to teach again.

The following is the statement that was read by my wife on the day of the sentencing.

> *We all have in mind that school should be a safe place for our children. High school is a stage in life, where we should have good memories, where you can remember those great friendships, instructors who inspired us and influenced our lives for good, activities such as school dances, prom, assemblies, performing arts, something that I really enjoyed, playing my violin. I think those should be the memories of every high school student, or at least that is how I would have loved to remember my high school years. Unfortunately, in my case I will remember my teacher, Mr. Hernandez, giving me alcohol, and forcefully convincing me to perform sexual acts that I didn't feel comfortable with and him urinating on me like a dog marking its territory.*
>
> *Mr. Hernandez, my music instructor, motivated me in learning music and lifted my self-esteem, but after he seduced me and after the sexual encounters, he would tell me many negative comments causing me to have low self-esteem. Mr. Hernandez manipulated me, giving him the power over my actions and having mental and emotional control over me. It got to the point where I was unable to make my own decisions. He made me feel like an unvalued object,*

dirty, and impotent. Mr. Hernandez deprived me from school events, friends and family.

After having the courage to expose Mr. Hernandez for his offense, I did not want to hear or talk about anything regarding the case. I felt confused and overwhelmed when I had to go through the whole criminal justice system, reliving and talking in front of many people in detail about what had happened. I became depressed; my depression took me to isolating myself from family, friends and also drop out school because I did not want any contact with anyone. I would spend hours crying, devastated due to what I was going through. I then realized that I needed professional help and decided to receive that help. It is extremely hard to grapple with the emotional and physical impact of the offense that Mr. Hernandez has done. Today the court has the opportunity to send a strong message, that this kind of conduct will not be tolerated from people in positions of trust.

Due to this situation, it tremendously impacted my wife's life as well as mine. It has helped us grow as individuals and together as a couple. We hold a strong bond of communication, and are able to trust and respect each other.

My wife has inspired me in many ways; she has awakened in me an inspiration to help others. I know that I would not have been able to deal with this challenge I faced in my life without the help and support that Kevin and others have given to me. I know for a fact that I have a purpose in life, and God is using me and my wife in unexplained but powerful ways.

Ramon Llerenas Story

Mario Torres had shared with us earlier this year the story about his cousin Ramon Llerenas Jr. who had been diagnosed with cancer. Agustin, Jennifer, Emir and I had the great opportunity to get to know Junior. I had never before met such a level-headed, mature individual. Junior was an exceptional son, brother, and friend. Junior had aspirations to complete college, and enjoyed a keen interest in film production. On Junior's 23rd birthday, Agustin, Jennifer and I had the privilege of sitting alongside Junior listening to his words of wisdom. Again, Junior was so content, with such confidence in his relationship with God. As long as he was close to the Lord, had his parents and friends nearby, everything else was insignificant.

During Junior's fight with cancer, he never became angry, but instead thanked God daily for his life and for his family. Never would you hear anything negative come from Junior. The words that he spoke were very deep. On a number of occasions, he came to our Sunday night gathering at my home, and his words always penetrated our hearts.

Last week Junior was told by doctors that he had only three months to live. Junior continued in his steady personality being thankful for each day, never showing any sign of bitterness. According to Mario, Junior began planning to do certain things that he wanted to do during his last days. We were scheduled to produce a video on Junior's life on December 20, 2007 at 5:00 PM. What blessed Junior the most was his family drawing so close together. At one point, Junior even said that if it took his life to bring about the drawing of his family closer to God, then so be it.

On December 20, 2007, Junior awoke to begin another day. He was not feeling well and began experiencing shortness of breath. His mom, dad, sisters, brother-in-law, and pastors were at his side and asked him if he wanted to go to the hospital, to which he said no, that he would be okay. They increased the level of his oxygen, and Junior said it helped. Junior's mom and dad began to realize he was not getting better.

They began to share with Junior what an incredible son he had always been, how he never got into trouble, and how incredibly proud they were of him for how courageous he had been over the past year. Junior would nod as they spoke their words of love to him, acknowledging that he understood. His parents began to sing songs to him and just held him. His mother told him it was okay for him to go, that they would be okay, and that they knew he would be with the Lord. At about 11:00 AM, during one such Spanish song which contained the words, "Go to Sleep," Junior took his last breath and went to sleep, to then awake to be with the Lord. We would not get the opportunity to produce a video of his life, but the impact he had on our lives will last forever.

In addition to this family tragedy, Junior's twenty year-old sister Natalie has recently been diagnosed with cancer as well. It is amazing how this family stands together in love and prayer, knowing that nothing happens outside of the control and direction of God.

Junior will always be an inspiration to all of us. His courage and confidence in his walk with the Lord will never be forgotten!

How does one make sense of these things? His mother was given the following passage from the Bible by her pastor:

The righteous pass away; the Godly often die before their time. And no one seems to care or wonder why. No one seems to understand that God is protecting them from the evil to come. For the Godly who die will rest in peace. Isa 57:1-2 NLT

This verse has become quite a comfort for Agustin, Jennifer, and many others. Junior wanted a career in Hollywood, and many were worried as to the temptations he might fall into if he would have moved to the Hollywood area.

There are certain things that we like to call "A God Thing." There have been so many times that we cannot believe how God intervenes and has His imprint on things around us. One example of a God thing is a person named Ellen Banks. I was privileged to meet Ellen back in the late 1980s. She is a medical doctor, and her husband is a professor at San Diego State University. They are two of the most humble people one could ever meet. I had not seen either of them for years. During a pre-planning meeting for an anti-violence march in memory of Javier Quiroz, I was standing at the site where he was gunned down. I saw a car go by, then pull over. This is in a rough part of town. An older woman got out, walking briskly toward me, and saying, "Kevin, how are you?" I was stunned because I had not seen here since the early 1990s. She said she recognized me from the street and wanted to say hello. She told me that she had a desire to reach out to the City Heights area, and began picking up children and taking them to her church for Sunday school. The main girl God had put a burden in her heart for was Alejandra, the little sister of Javier Quiroz and Agustin Pena. What are the odds on this? I explained what I was involved with, and she explained that her church felt a burden to help the young people in this area as well.

In addition, another individual by the name of Curt Dokken of World Impact had moved to the area long before Javier was killed. He too had a burden in his heart to reach out to this community and even moved here with his wife and daughter. Again, what are the odds of a number of people having a similar burden, some of whom never knew each other, and others having not had contact with them in so many years? These are God things that we just have to be awed by and realize that God knows what He is doing.

CHAPTER 7

▼

DEVELOPMENT
STRATEGIES

Genuine change generally occurs in an environment of unconditional love and acceptance. Often people tell me how fortunate I am to have such great friends. I remind them that to have great friends, you must first be a great friend.

Continually reinforce that your mentee has the same potential to impact others as you have on him or her. We have to fight the mentality that the mentee feels where they feel like a pet project of yours. They must see the vision of leading others. They were impacted, and now they must impact others as well.

We must daily check our motives, making sure we are not fostering quid-pro-quo (or this-for-that) mentorship, which can be undermining and extremely destructive. We must make sure we are not drawing self-worth from individuals we are mentoring.

It is crucial that we seek to influence but do not allow the mentee to have influence over us. It is important to fill the void in our lives with a support system that is set up around us via peers, not mentees. The reason I bring this up is because it is very emotionally draining to mentor people. We can be drawn into unhealthy relationships if we are not careful. In addition, the mentee can become very manipulative and have their mentor wrapped around their little finger.

I primarily use intrinsic motivation strategies, with very little extrinsic strategies. My reason for this is because extrinsic strategies can be easily manipulated because they are based on tangibles. Intrinsic strategies are based on deeply held beliefs. I have found that I help the mentee become grounded in a belief that they are in this world for a specific purpose and that they are needed to help others; it drives their sense of purpose, which we all long for.

We must learn to discipline ourselves so we develop a mindset in which we see the best in others as opposed to seeing their worst. It is common for people to always focus on the negative. We must train ourselves to see people for their greatness. I remember a news story about our program when I was in the police department. The reporter said that the young people we were mentoring were no angels, but that off-duty police officer Kevin LaChapelle treats them all as if they were.

We must be committed to being strategic in every statement and action taken. Our actions have serious consequences, both positive and negative. Every word we say or action we take sends a message to our mentee. For example, my words can build up or tear down more so than I may want to admit. I also have the power to praise too much, which can lead to enabling the mentee to become cocky and over-confident.

One of the dilemmas a mentee faces each day is that "This is too good to be true!" Having said this, we must never forget to under-promise and over-deliver in all relationships. The worst-case scenario is one in which you promise something to your mentee and fail to deliver. Your credibility is perhaps the strongest asset you have in developing a mentee. It is your commitment to consistency that your mentee probably lacked all of their life.

The mentor must act like a mentor. Often the mentor thinks he or she must act like the mentee to reach them. This could not be further from the truth. For example, in the police department I would hear police officers talking gang slang to gang members and even referring to them by their gang monikers. I made it a point to never, ever dignify their destructive lifestyle by calling them by their gang nicknames or fall into the gang lingo. It is crucial that you establish yourself with credibility to your mentee. If you are not even sure what you stand for, how can you possibly help the mentee learn what they should stand for? Having a command presence about oneself in strong mentoring relationships is essential. The same goes for a parenting relationship. Have you ever asked yourself how parents can quickly forget that they are parents and instead treat their children like their buddies? Although it is important to develop positive relationships, the key is that a mentor is developing the mentee into a positive, results-driven life. Never should the mentor conform to the mentee's negative lifestyle.

For a mentor to really be successful, the mentor must be driven by something outside of himself/herself as to why they want to lead others. This is a huge factor in what motivates us. If we are just looking for friends, or looking for people to control, we are playing with fire. The only legitimate reason to mentor others is to pass on positive characteristics to another. The most fundamental question you must ask yourself is why you want to lead others. Many have ulterior motives to fulfill their own self-worth, to provide power and control of others, or to simply feed their own insecurities.

The reality is that we should want to lead others because we want to do the right thing and have a positive impact on the lives of others. What we get in return is seeing people change their lives and knowing we were instrumental in that change. We see our own purpose in life by impacting others and making a difference.

Last, a serious development strategy to consider is that it is crucial to ensure that we build resiliency in our mentee. For example, we have to assume that at times our mentee will stray off course. How well can we develop them enough so that they can quickly find their way back? Often when a mentor does not hear from a mentee, it is due to their straying off track. Isolating themselves from us is primarily due to feeling bad for letting us down, and knowing that when they see us, we will address the very issues they may not want to hear.

Let's discuss an example of a development strategy for gang intervention which I have used in the past successfully, and still use today. This gang intervention strategy can work as a model for a number of different circumstances. The first thing I had to do was determine and isolate what the problem behavior was. I would hear from community members that they were witnessing negative behavior from gang members, which gave a negative perception of the gang members, causing people to distance themselves from helping the gang members.

When I looked at some of the causes for the negative behavior, I found inconsistent zero-tolerance policies within the schools, the family, and the places the young people would congregate, such as malls. In addition, the gang members were experiencing inconsistent consequences for their actions, which really was due to poor collaboration between law enforcement agencies and schools, as well as a lack of community involvement. Last, the gang members were lacking a positive common direction for their lives.

Much of these negative behaviors were due to a dysfunctional family model that offered little or no support system for them. Many households had one parent rather than two. This posed a dilemma, because a two-parent home offers much more stability for children. For example, in a two-parent family model, one parent can be a disciplinarian, while the other acts as a nurturer. The parents may swap roles here and there, but the key is that someone is providing structure, while the other provides the nurturing. This is perhaps the most vital part of mentoring. We use this with many of our mentees in which we strategize on a team approach to the mentoring process. For example, one mentor can focus on the discipline, while another can focus on the nurturing. In other cases, one mentor can act as a discipliner and nurturer, however this can be less effective.

The following diagrams illustrate the family model and how the breakdown of the two parent family has caused government agencies and community based organizations to step in to help to fill the void.

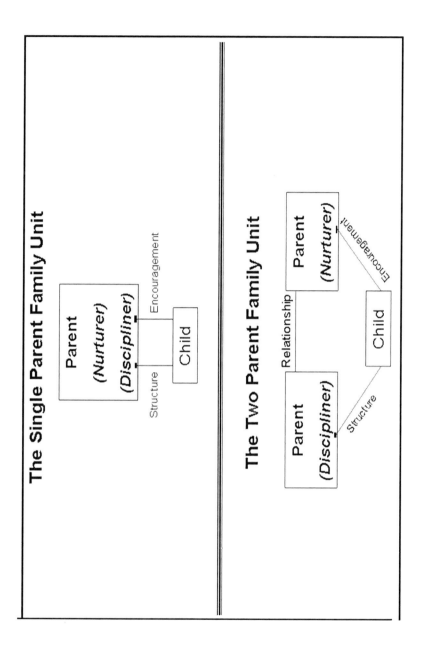

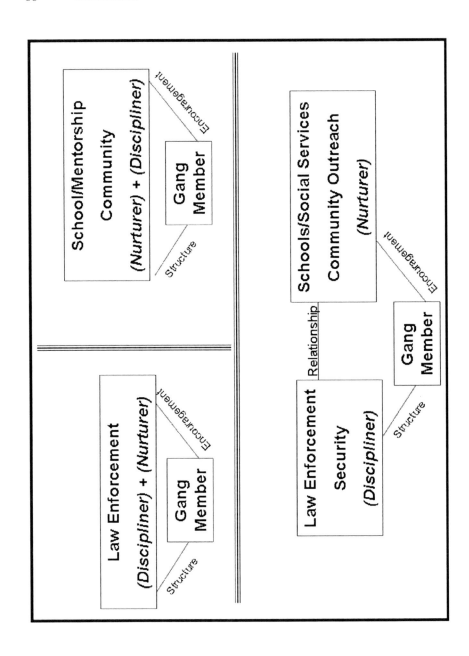

When the family support system fails, the criminal justice system must now deal with the problem of a gang member who is engaging in criminal behavior. Still, it is essential that the two components of discipline and nurture are both a part of the solution. For example, the police can provide the discipline, while the school must take up the nurturer's role. Just as parents communicate with each other, so also must agencies communicate.

We can see the effectiveness of a functional family model and apply the same principles to other programs that are in place because of the decline of the family unit.

Let's examine the psychology of gang members. They have a desire for a purpose. However, instead of a purpose for good, gangs have corrupted their purpose for bad. They have a desire to be loved and accepted; however, instead of love from family, they find a distorted love and coerced acceptance in the gang. They desire to be a part of something, but instead of being part of something positive, they become a part of at least something, even though it is negative. So for a program to be effective, it must contain each of the components that the functional family model would have provided.

In addition, there must be an integrated solution. If the gang member is in the middle, all of the support agencies must be in sync around the gang member. Police, district attorneys, parole and probation, social services, schools, community-based organizations, churches, and families all must work hand in hand. The more united these groups are, the tighter the support system for the gang member.

Gang members have high manipulation skills; therefore, they will have a tendency to turn each of the above-mentioned groups against each other, just as children will turn mom against dad in order to get their own way.

When we examine the characteristics of gang members, we see that they have a desire to instill fear and intimidation in others. By instilling fear and intimidation, the gang member feels empowered. If we can transition this corrupted sense of self-worth into a system of leading others to a positive way of life, they can receive the same feeling of self-worth, but with positive consequences. The family life is a huge issue. Many times parents enable their kids, or are absent or naïve in allowing the gang member to go unchecked. We as a community fail kids in low-income areas, resulting often in the kids not being given the choice to resist gangs out of fear of retaliation for not joining up. Sadly, many agencies have abdicated their role to protect the youth.

The behavior patterns we see in gangs are generally gathering in groups to intimidate, having violent tendencies, and looking for potential opportunities to commit crimes such as carjacking, robberies, assaults, and narcotics. A community must ask itself whether gang activity is what it wants its community members to see as a way of life?

If we say no, we must recognize that establishing standards with regard to behaviors is key. For example, who wants to take their kids to the mall when gang members or young people exhibiting negative behaviors, and begin harassing you and your family? Rules without relationships lead to rebellion. Values and integrity must be taught and modeled through mentorship, especially once a young person has reached a certain level of rebelliousness.

Communities must encourage and support those willing to serve their communities. We have the opportunity to empower others or destroy their efforts and effectiveness! If we don't reach the inner-city kids, the gangs will! Often I have talked to non-profit organizations that feel undermined instead of empowered by local police. There must be a shift in mindset on the part of all social service agencies.

For intervention strategies to be effective, they must include zero-tolerance, a targeting of the negative behavior, an empowering of the community by supporting them instead of the gangs, maintaining a firm approach, disrupting gang activities by utilizing all available resources, and empowering the families when possible. It is said that a child left to himself brings shame to his mother, and this could not be more true than with a gang member. Most gang members are looking for a leader; if they do not see positive role models, they will succumb to the negative gang leaders.

You must ask yourself what you are doing to make a difference. If you are a police chief, police officer, probation officer, district attorney, social worker, school teacher, mentor, or whatever, why are you in the position you are in? Are you purpose-and results-driven? Have you become cynical? Are you empowering others or hindering their efforts? Are you enabling negative behavior? Use your position for good; do not become cynical and stagnant. Others are desperately relying upon your position to empower them.

Chapter 8

▼

Seek to Empower, Not Control

How do we obtain a mindset that pushes us to empower others instead of control them? We see this frequently in a parent who pushes their child in a particular direction in which the child has no interest. I have seen young people go through college, then after graduation realize they have no drive to be in the profession they were pushed into by their parents. Often parents vicariously live through their children and push them in a direction that they may have wished they had gone in. This is very destructive.

We have to get to a point in which we have a perspective of understanding that we cannot control destiny, *per se.* For example, I believe God has gifted each of us with a particular gift that we can use for the good of others. If I help a person to seek and find that gift, which in turn helps them clarify their mission in  life whereby they can begin to make decisions, I have done well. However, if I begin to tell the mentee what I believe they should do in life, it is in direct conflict with their choosing their own direction in life.

This can be very tough. When a mentee begins to chart their course in life, we want so much to control them. The reality is that we cannot. The more we push, the more they will rebel.

In 1998 during my last year on an elected school board, I was feeling very beaten up. I had a lot of questions about life and about my direction for the future. One day I drove through a drive-through Jack in the Box restaurant in San Diego. I met a young man named Jose Orozco, who later would have the most impact on my life than anyone ever has.

While at this Jack in the Box waiting for my order, I began to ask Jose the same questions I ask people when I am trying to provoke them into changing the direction of their lives. I asked him if he planned to go to college, to which he responded that he had dropped out of high school. He was 17 years old and felt if he worked hard, he could become a shift leader at the fast-food restaurant in about six months.

I saw Jose on a few more occasions, and each time inquired as to what was happening in his life. I would encourage him to go back to school and get his G.E.D. At the time, I was travelling around the country doing speaking engagements. On several occasions Jose would call me and we would talk about life and the consequences of our decisions. At one point Jose told me about his mother who had died of cancer when he was young. A few years later his father died of cancer as well. Jose was tossed to and fro from relative to relative, from Mexico to the United States. He would tell me that he wanted to become an attorney. I would always encourage him that he could do it if he set his mind on it.

There was something very different about Jose. He and I had a connection that was amazing. We just clicked. He did not realize it, but God would actually use him to shape my life more than ever. Jose thought I was there to mentor him, yet in many ways he mentored me. Jose went back to school and obtained his G.E.D. He then registered for San Diego City College. Upon completion, he enrolled at San Diego State University. He sought a double major in philosophy and political science. I was so blessed to attend his graduation.

Jose is now in his last year of law school at California Western School of Law. The journey we have travelled together has had a major impact on both our lives. Along the way, however, there were many times I wanted to tell him what decision he should make. Even now, there are things I hear and see and I say, "No Jose, do it this way," or that way. I have to keep coming back to the fact that Jose is in charge of his own life. It is his life, not mine. I have to be very careful, because I too wanted to go to law school; however, I did not do well on the L.S.A.T. exam, so was not able to enroll. I have to constantly check myself, making sure I am not trying to vicariously live my own life through Jose's life.

For me, I have to entrust Jose to God. I have strong faith in God and believe He has Jose in His grip. Now if I genuinely believe that, I have to let go. Letting go is perhaps the hardest part of mentorship. We want to protect the mentee, making sure all of their decisions are the best. We undermine their ability to grow by not allowing them to make their own mistakes. As hard as it is, we have to let go, and for me I have to let God take charge. I have to pray for Jose daily, and just be there if he ever needs a pillar to lean on.

Last week I had the honor of speaking at California Western School of Law on the topic of Mentorship and Community Service. It was incredible to share Jose's story with people who did not realize how far he had come along in his life.

Here is a note from Jose and what Mentorship has meant to him:

You only get a chance like this once in a lifetime. You buy tickets every week and then wait anxiously for the next day to see if you hit the jackpot. I didn't win the lottery that night but I also didn't buy a lottery ticket either. In fact I never bought one. That night, however, was my luckiest day. I was working at a Jack in the Box in North Park. I was fairly new on the job and was just getting the hang of things. While taking orders at the register, a group of people walked in. "Big deal, huh," groups of people always walk into a

Jack in the Box. Oh no, these were not just any group of individuals, with them was a special person, one whom only God knew would change me forever.

Kevin LaChapelle and his friends walked in to have dinner. They played a joke on me. Kevin was playing around making jokes. A few minutes after they left, I received a call from Jack. At the end of the conversation Jack was being impersonated by Kevin. He told me that if I ever wanted to hang out with them to give him a call and gave me his phone number. I had seen Kevin before when he would come through the drive-thru and ask me questions about my life and if I wanted to go to college.

During that time of my life, I was going through very dark days. I had recently dropped out of high school and was just beginning my life as an adult but quickly realized that working at a Jack in the Box was not something I wanted to do for the rest of my life.

A few weeks later, we went to a rappelling trip, and soon afterwards we became regular acquaintances. We went to lunch every once in a while and discussed many things about life and the world. I realized that the world was bigger than what I thought it was. This is the problem with young people who are convinced that reality is their life in gangs, violence, and/or drugs. They do not know that the world is bigger than that.

On one occasion, Kevin gave me a gift for my birthday, a Bible. Even though I had grown up Catholic and went to Church every Sunday as a young child, I did not believe much in the religion itself. The timing of the Bible was perfect. As mentioned before, I was going through very dark days. I began to submerge myself in the Bible and realized many things about our relation to God. I found many inconsistencies about Church and God Himself. For example, churches depend on a few spiritual leaders who then guide the rest of the church. The Bible, however, tells the individual to seek God Himself and not others to guide them to him. This might just show what condition our society is in when individuals seek the church to get to God, when in fact all they need to do is seek God. I am not denying the importance of accountability or of a support system, but am discrediting the dependence some people place on someone else's faith.

Kevin and I debated on many things about the Bible, and there were times where I would accept his argument and there were others where he seemed to agree with me. It seemed as though as my relationship with Kevin was growing, so was with my relationship with God. I am not implying in any way that Kevin is the way to God but that God sent me a good friend such as Kevin.

Up to this day I always consider myself an extremely fortunate person to have met Kevin. I am convinced that God crossed our paths so that we can together live this life which at times seems so useless. Everywhere one turns there is corruption. Many believe that we have the best government system in the world. I would argue that any government system which is governed by humans is corrupt. There is no surprise then, that Kevin has seen and exposed corrupt systems in our government.

We would like to believe that things will get better in our nation. This, however, will not happen until, like Kevin, others rise up to expose and change the current corrupt systems. The status quo is strong because just like the young people who are convinced that their world is a reality in which they cannot get out, we at times are also convinced that ours is reality, and that there is no other. It is up to you and me to decide what our future reality will be.

After having shared so much with my sister Leslie about different mentoring experiences such as with Jose, she began sharing with her perspective on mentoring. She had attended an alternative education program in high school that illustrates  the mentor relationship perfectly. Note that when Leslie talks about leaders seeing the best in them, it is consistent with what our approach has been for years. My sister's story is a good example of why it is so important to empower rather than control. Here is her perspective:

There are so many creative and unconventional ways to mentor, sometimes it needs to be, as was in my case, or it never would have worked for me. I was a fifteen year old, mean, angry, cold hearted, rebellious, hard-to-deal-with teenager, getting enrolled at Pace, an alternative high school in Denver, with my mother and Sister Kathleen, the nun who ran the school. I absolutely did not want to be there. I wanted to be in a big school where I could blend in and no one would notice when I skipped classes, which was so much more fun than sitting in a stuffy classroom with a bunch of nerds, jocks, and teachers who thought they had the right to tell me what to do. I hated school, teachers and anyone in authority. I hated being told what to do, and what I hated even worse was the expectations adults placed upon me. Nope, this school was not my thing. Way too small. And another nun, no way was I going to deal with that too! But my mom had heard about it and thought it would be just what

I and the whole family needed to straighten me up so I would fly right, as mom used to always tell me. But I had it all figured out.

With my smart tongue and hateful attitude, Sister Kathleen would see that this was no place for a girl like me, and she'd tell my mom and I that we needed to move on and find somewhere else to go. I knew how to push adults' buttons and make them despise and cringe at me, especially nuns, since I went to Catholic schools my whole life. This was easy as pie. Without wasting any time, I let her have every bit of my hatefulness and bitterness towards her school, the Catholic religion and anything else I could throw out there. I'd embarrass my mom more than I ever had before, just to get back at her for making me go. Purposely, I was definitely at my worst. But instead of the usual reaction of disgust and insult that I fully expected, because I brought it out in all adults, especially nuns, she gently said, "Leslie, I see you don't have a strong Catholic faith, and I want you to know that's okay, honey, there are many other ways to understand God." She asked me if she found someone to teach a class in Comparison Religions, would I commit to going to each class and working on my relationship with God. I was astounded! She stopped me dead in my tracks, which wasn't easy to do. I think she was the only adult who didn't take me personally and feel offended by my attitude.

She seemed to see right through me, that I actually craved a close intimate relationship with God. She acted like she loved me and my open and frank opinions! She actually validated me and my feelings. Wow! Yes, I told her I would commit to going to a class like that. I had never thought about other religions or other ways to relate to God. She made me feel so good, like she was accepting what I felt in my heart and soul, even though I never saw anything good in it. As much as she respected me, I knew it would be easy for me to respect her too. She planted a tiny little seed in me that day that lasted a lifetime. In my eyes, she was my first true mentor. But she wasn't the traditional mentor who followed up and encouraged me that year. I didn't want that. I wanted to be left alone by her, to prove to her and myself that I could do it without any help. She did leave me alone. She never asked questions, never checked up on me, never did anything but greet me every morning and accept me like she did everyone else at that school. I needed that. I loved that. She made my favorite saying so true: "Treat everyone as if they're good, because they will live up to, or down to, your expectations of them." I was absolutely going to let my good side out; if she saw it, I knew it had to be somewhere in me. I had two weeks to wait until the first day of school, and I could not believe it, but I actually was really looking forward to it.

On that first day of school, twenty-eight of us troubled kids, who couldn't make it in a regular school, five advisors, and Sister Kathleen, sat in a big circle. She explained what was ahead for the coming year. First the rules. (Here we go, I thought). No fighting and no put-downs. Hmm, that was it? Nothing about ditching? Cool! That's easy enough. Next, the advisors. They were not teachers, they were advisors, they said, to advise us. They were on the same level as we were, so we were to call them by their first names, just as they called us by our first names. We could all learn from each other. (Cool, I could deal with that!) Then one of the advisors spoke up. She said they were here to teach us whatever we wanted to learn. If we didn't show up for class, which meant we didn't want to learn, the advisors would find a new job where they were needed and wanted.

So, what do we want to learn? What would keep us coming to school every day? Sister Kathleen spoke up first. She asked who would like to take a class in Comparative Religions. Most of us raised our hands. One of the advisors volunteered to teach the class. Another advisor asked if any of us would be interested in a class he would love to teach, Eastern Religions, Philosophies and Meditations. He said he had been studying it, and would love to teach us what he'd been learning. Again, most of us raised our hands. Sister Kathleen told us that she noticed a lot of us had a hard time communicating our feelings in healthy ways, and that we could use a class to help us with that. After some brainstorming, we came up with a class called Discussions and Debates, and one of the advisors volunteered to teach that.

The day went on like this for six hours. We created all kinds of fun classes that we really wanted to learn, that made school worth getting up for. Like Organics and Gardening, Yoga and Fitness, Comparison Shopping and Budgeting, and Family Planning and Values. Some of us wanted to go to college, so needed credits in regular classes, like Math, Science and English. Some of these would tie into the classes we already chose. For the rest, we had advisors who were willing to help us individually, with what we needed and wanted.

Each advisor was assigned five or six of us, to be our own personal advisor. They kept a close eye on us and our progress. For an English credit, we were all expected to keep a journal that would be shared only with our advisor, whom we quickly learned, was our mentor. The mentors were the ones to follow up and give us the support and encouragement we needed on a daily basis. They got to know us as intimately as we would allow.

For my mentor Betty, it wasn't easy. I had lots of tall, thick walls built solidly, top, bottom and all around me. I never let anyone in. She saw this, and never pushed. She let me be as shut down as I needed. By her accepting me as I was, it helped me to peel back some of those thick layers of walls, slowly at first. She saw my hatred and hostility. She saw my unhappiness with my home life. Rather than push me, she saw that I needed some history credits to get through the year. She gave me a most creative assignment that made everything change for me. I had to spend a month making a report of my parents' history, learning why they were like they were, learning their backgrounds and family life. With that assignment, and the help of my Comparison Religions and Eastern Religions and Philosophy classes, I felt an overwhelming sense of love, compassion and forgiveness for my parents. I finally realized that they weren't here to make my life as miserable as they possibly could, that they really were only doing the best they knew how, because of the lives they had led and the way they had been raised.

It all came together for me, all my scattered puzzle pieces to life finally all fit, and I could see the big picture, so plainly too. Everything became clear to me. I learned that no matter how bad we think things are, they come from God, so it's really all good if we would just open our minds and see it that way. I saw what the true meanings of 'Every dark cloud has a silver lining,' 'What comes around goes around,' and what 'Cause and Effect' really mean. I realized God needed me to go through the tough times, because he needed me to be strong for unforeseen things down the road. He had big plans for me. How exciting was that! I started embracing my pains and troubles, because I knew they were for the good, somehow … I didn't know how, but I had so much faith and understanding of God now that I knew it would be okay. I started looking forward to my life and growing older and wiser.

Betty and the other advisors were traditional mentors. They're the ones who encouraged us, never gave up on us, never judged or left us. They were there any time we needed them. They even gave us all their home phone numbers and we were told we were welcome to call any time, day or night, if we needed help with anything. We could trust them with anything. They never betrayed or broke our trust. All of us 'problem' kids ended that year as completely different people. It's hard to believe, but a couple of the kids were even more difficult than I was! But in the end, we were all filled with love for ourselves, our families, the world and each other. We all couldn't wait to get out in the world and learn even more. We all learned we had a purpose in life and how we fit into this huge, confusing world. We learned to respect people, animals and nature, as they are all parts of God. We all learned what we put out, we get back.

I can't speak for the rest of them, but for me, I ended up embracing and accepting the Catholic religion, and all religions. I realized it's the people that make religions bad, not the religions themselves. I learned to love all the differences in people and their faiths. I saw that since we are all from God, we all have good in us. What was important, like Pace did for me, was to ignore the bad and bring out the good in others. I realized that people aren't 'bad,' they're merely the products of what life has dealt them, their upbringing, and the choices they have made. I was in awe at the way this world God had created was so perfectly in order. The good and bad of it all worked together. The way everything and everyone fell together for reasons only God knew was incredible to me. I was actually finally happy to be alive and excited about all the mysteries of the world. My mind and heart opened up like I never knew it could. But it wasn't because of me, or the classes I took, even though that was a big part of it. The main thing was because of the way I was treated. I got respect, so gave it. It was that simple. Sister Kathleen listened and accepted me, so I was able to do the same for her and her school. Betty accepted me and the way I was, so I accepted her and her help and was able to let my guard down and soften my heart. As soon as my heart changed, so did my life. Daily, I started seeing God working. I saw so many miracles, not only in my own life but also in the lives of others and in the world. I saw God's hand in everyone, everything and everywhere. I saw everything in a whole new light.

Pace made a huge difference for me, so when I left, I knew I wanted to keep growing and helping others like I had been helped. I couldn't wait to see what God had in store for me. I opened myself up to Him and said, "Here I am Lord, do with me what you will!" I was so filled with love for myself and love for life that I was excited to share it with whoever needed it. I found others who needed it through my jobs, friends, family and even strangers I would meet. Sometimes it was as small as a smile or a hug for someone who looked mean and mad at the world. Sometimes I would run into people who needed more, like an ear or a shoulder. Some wanted even more than that, like advice and input. Others needed a true friend, someone to stick by them and be there, no matter what. I have always made sure I was available to whoever needed it. I'm so grateful for what Pace gave me. Never do I forget why I am where I am today. That's my gift back to Pace and the world.

A close friend whom I have mentored over the years is Aimee Millensifer. Here is what our mentoring relationship has meant to her:

Leslie has been a good lifelong friend who has mentored me my whole life. She's solid as a rock, firm and never wavers. Because of this, I consider her my Rock of Gibraltar. I can always call on her to vent or complain, and no matter how busy she is, she has always made time for me. She has never judged me. She always brings everything back to God, which is the core of everything. She has so much love, tolerance and compassion. Mentoring is a relationship that goes deeper than friendship. Mentoring means to allow time, grace and patience for the mentee to find their way with direction. We can't force people to change, or turn from their negative behavior such as using drugs or alcohol. But we have to lead by example, be a sounding board, and be able to relate to any subject. Sometimes we have to mentor our friends, without them even knowing what we are doing. We have to be true to ourselves so we can be true to others, that is the mark of a true mentor.

▼

CHAPTER 9

BUILDING A POWERMENTOR SUPPORT SYSTEM

A great example of mentorship is Jesus' private time with His disciples. This exemplifies the type of relationship we must have with our mentees. We must have the ability to network our life into the fabric of those we mentor.

When Agustin's little brother Javier was killed, right away Agustin and I knew very well what God would ask of us. We were to lead Javier's friends. The strongest love we could ever demonstrate to Javier would be to be committed to his friends. We would commit ourselves to be there for his friends as we had hoped to be there for Javier himself.

During the funeral service, it became evident that God would bond us closely with Javier's best friends. God used the grieving process to knit our hearts together with theirs. For the week during his funeral and burial, we would be together almost non-stop. Most of the time words never were spoken, just tears. We wept with them over the loss of Javier.

Javier was buried on Thursday, and that following Sunday, we met with Javier's friends. There were about 15 of them present. We created a notebook for each of them which contained a picture of Javier with the words, "In Loving Memory of Javier Quiroz. The next page had the following verses:

> *The LORD replied, "If you return to me, I will restore you so you can continue to serve me. If you speak words that are worthy, you will be my spokesman. You are to influence them; do not let them influence you! They will fight against you like an attacking army, but I will make you as secure as a fortified wall. They will not conquer you, for I will protect and deliver you. I, the LORD, have spoken! Yes, I will certainly keep you safe from these wicked men. I will rescue you from their cruel hands."*
> *-Jer 15:19-21*
>
> *Where there is ignorance of God, crime runs wild; but what a wonderful thing it is for a nation to know and keep his laws.—Prov 29:18*
>
> *The LORD is for me, so I will not be afraid. What can mere mortals do to me? Yes, the LORD is for me; he will help me. I will look in triumph at those who hate me. It is better to trust the LORD than to put confidence in people.—Ps 118:6-8*
>
> *The eyes of the LORD search the whole earth in order to strengthen those whose hearts are fully committed to him. What a fool you have been! From now on, you will be at war."—2 Chron 16:9-10*
>
> *So let us go out to him outside the camp and bear the disgrace he*

bore. For this world is not our home; we are looking forward to our city in heaven, which is yet to come.—Heb 13:13-14

Behold, the whirlwind of the LORD Goes forth with fury, a continuing whirlwind; It will fall violently on the head of the wicked. The fierce anger of the LORD will not return until He has done it, And until He has performed the intents of His heart. In the latter days you will consider it.—Jer 30:23-24

And he will turn the hearts of the fathers to the children, and the hearts of the children to their fathers, lest I come and strike the earth with a curse."—Mal 4:6

On the first page of the notebook, we had them write a letter to Javier. In this letter we asked them to tell Javier whatever was in their hearts. We also asked them to make some commitments to Javier with regards to decisions they would make in their life.

One by one, we went around asking them to read their letter aloud. It was remarkable. All of them had basically told Javier they loved and missed him, and that they were so sorry for what had happened. Then they began to share with him that they knew he would want them to do better in school and obey their parents. They began to commit to Javier that they wanted something better in life. They  were committed to doing better in school and listening to their teachers.

Prior to this, many of them had contemplated dropping out of school as it was a difficult task to continue. They now were making commitments that before they had never thought of.

We then asked them to write down their weaknesses and what could hinder them meeting their goals. They then jotted down some core values that they all agreed to hold each other accountable to as a group. Some of these core values were that they would encourage each other to make better decisions, and that they would consider consequences before making decisions.

We then set a weekly meeting time and have been doing so ever since. This is indicative of a good support system. In addition we have been developing them to mentor their younger brothers, sisters, neighbors and others. Now they are seeing the impact they can have on those around them, just as they have experienced the impact we have had on them.

We took this group of thirty-seven on an outing to Yosemite National Park. It was incredible to see their excitement and reflections of their life. Javier had gone on the same trip the previous year, so this was dedicated to his memory.

Many young people have had to learn the hard way that they seriously need a support system. Sometimes pride gets in the way of acknowledging one's need for support. Such was the case for Miguel Samaniego. Miguel and I have an incredible friendship. Miguel is one of the most genuine individuals I've ever known. He has been a great inspiration and encouragement to me and has become one of my best friends. Never do you hear Miguel speak negatively about others. Instead, Miguel challenges people when they are gossiping and encourages them to see the good in others. I have learned a lot from Miguel. His courage at such a young age to raise his children is phenomenal. When so many young men abdicate their role as fathers, Miguel lets go of his own dreams so his children's dreams can one day become their reality. Here is his perspective of what has transpired in his life.

Miguel's Story

Many questions have arisen in my head for the past four years. How do I become the father my children deserve? How will I guide my kids through life? As well as many miscellaneous questions that come along with being a father. Perhaps every man by instinct knows what to do with the experiences he encounters throughout life. One will ask when is the perfect age to

take on this responsibility of becoming a father. If we where to ask a large number of people, many would have mixed feelings about the topic. I'm pretty sure many would respond that the perfect time to take on the responsibility of becoming a father is when a man is financially secure, has the maturity to teach the child the principles of life, and has a spouse at his side that has faith in him to protect his family.

I am far from being a perfect role model. I became a father at age seventeen. Most would agree that a seventeen year old is hardly prepared for fatherhood. I was a senior in high school when I received the news. Panic and fear rushed through my veins. I had no idea what I had gotten myself into. The world had fallen on my shoulders and my dreams had been shattered. Everyone around me, including my loved ones, looked down on me as if I had shamed the family. My actions not only affected me but also my mother. She was the gossip of everyone's conversation, and many criticized her. My heart was broken when I saw my mom's hand tremble, and she broke down in tears as I told her the news. That's when all the questions began to haunt me.

What was I thinking? Should I run as far as I could and never look back? Not only would this have caused my mother more pain but also would have affected that child's life so that he would view the world without a father. That's when I realized that I had to take on the responsibilities of becoming the father whom a child would desire and admire. How would I begin to take on the role of a father? My life had shifted 360 degrees all in a blink of an eye! I had to make drastic changes in my life in order to prepare myself for a child. I began by isolating myself from negative influences, including some loved ones. I figured I would resolve my problems on my own. I thought that hearing advice from people would only stir my mind into greater depression, but I was wrong!

I needed someone; a peer, a mentor, someone that would encourage me to continue on with my legacy. Pretending to solve all my problems on my own only caused more frustration and anger towards life and the people I loved the most. Asking for advice from someone is nothing to be ashamed of. I had to put my pride aside and admit that sharing my struggles with someone lifted a whole lot of weight from my shoulders. That someone was a generous person by the name of Kevin LaChapelle. His wisdom and love towards others impacted me in a way that I had never experienced. He opened my eyes to a new world full of hope and possibilities. All I needed was the courage and dedication to make a difference in my children's life. I have nothing to prove to others, my goal in life is to prove to myself that anything is possible, that the "sky is the limit." I need to be a mentor and a role model for my kids.

Sometimes you need to fall and kiss the asphalt to realize how important it is to make a wise decision in the moment that matters. One must realize that a simple mistake of pleasure can change your life drastically. I can't blame anyone but myself. I knew exactly what I was doing. For teens who are actively involved in sexual relationships, I ask you to consider the problems of getting a girl pregnant at a young age and catching a sexually transmitted disease. The best thing to do is not have sex until you are married. I know that sounds corny to most guys out there, but trust me, don't set yourself up for failure. As time has passed by I think to myself, *what if?* What if I had made better decisions, I wouldn't be dealing with the issue of raising kids without having gone to college to be in a better financial condition. Where would I be if I were single and had two kids? Would I still be striving for my goal in life of becoming an architect? Would I still be enrolled in college? Like I have said, many questions will remain unanswered, and only more questions will cross my mind. Don't get me wrong, I love my kids more than anything, and I would do anything in the world to be with them. Come to think about it, they have been the best thing that God could have ever given me in this world. It's simply another reason to keep on fighting to succeed in life. I'm aware that I'm not the first or last teen parent in the world. I just hope that my thoughts and feelings could impact teens to be more responsible in the decisions they make. For those who are teen parents, know that the child is not to blame, and it takes a real man to face the consequences. Only a coward would run away, ignoring his responsibilities. I understand that a man has the right to be happy, but don't be selfish! That child has the right to be loved by the ones who brought him or her into this world.

Statistically, most teenage parents who try to make things work out fail and go their separate ways. The few who do make it can truly understand the value of sticking together through the good and bad times. So be wise and know that the only person you should be sexually active with should be your partner for life! Sex is not a game. Young people play the game of who can get laid the most, not realizing how complex things will be, and not understanding that you should not be having sex at an early age. But then again, what do I know.

My oldest child is only four. The brain is still like a sponge, absorbing information from his surroundings. They are much smarter than you think. They can sense when things are going bad between their parents. The hardest issue I have is how to protect him from all the evil in the world. I don't want to be to over-protective because I'm afraid he will rebel at a certain point in life. What can I do? He is ready to start school, and I'm terrified he might fight with others or will be rude to the teacher. I don't want the school to think that is what I'm teaching him. I have been raised the old-fashioned way: If I misbehaved, I would get a spanking. Nowadays you cannot even discipline your child that way. I guess you are as good of a parent as the effort you put into it. I believe a spanking in the behind wouldn't do the child any harm as long as you maintain control and explain why he is getting punished. I let him know every day how much I love him. I guess I'll be just as excited and nervous as he will be the first day of school. There are endless possibilities of things out in the world that can harm my son when I'm not around, and I'm afraid, but I guess you can't think negatively and always have to have faith and trust in God.

My younger child is two. She is a sweetheart. A petite girl, as if she were only eleven months old. I hate to say it, but she is a mama's girl. That is another thing that bothers me, feeling that sometimes I don't dedicate as much time to them as I want. I'm always working, and when I'm home I want to rest. I wish I were a superhero to maintain my strength at work and come home and play all night with them. I am aware that I'm working my tail off to give them a better way of life. Anyway, back to my little girl; thinking ahead, she is going to drive me crazy when she starts dating. The only good thing is that I won't have to worry for another twenty years! I'll be lucky if she reaches eighteen before dating. How can I make her understand that most guys in their teen years will only use her and manipulate her? For now she is my little angel who lights up my day. Her precious smile, a bright Colgate smile with a gap between her front teeth makes me the luckiest man in the world.

As for me, I am twenty-two years old and shooting for the stars. Throughout my life I have had many mentors that have opened their hearts to reach out to me. I'm very thankful for every single one of them and want them to know that they have captured a piece of my heart. This just shows how much the art of mentoring can impact the life of a person, helping them make wise decisions, and know if I do make a mistake, which we all do, will have the capacity to step up to the plate and face the consequences. We can all learn from each other and make things better.

I can go on to naming the people who have helped me out, but I would like to mention three very important people. Kevin, whom I consider my best friend, still gives me advice to this day. The second one is my high school soccer coach Jon Beaubien, who kept me out of trouble, and his presence encouraged me to try harder not only in sports but also in school. And last but not least Miss Abalos, an elementary school teacher who opened up her heart to me when I first arrived in this country. She started teaching me the complex English language. She encouraged me when others made fun of me for my poor language skills. My heart goes out to all of those special souls, those PowerMentors!

CHAPTER 10

▼

MULTI-LEVEL MENTORING

Multi-level marketing is not what I am talking about here. Multi-level mentoring is the basic pass-it-on philosophy. As we discussed earlier in this book, each of us not only needs to be led, but also we need to lead others. When a person has an impact on another, it impacts that person significantly. I cannot count how many others I have mentored, where I grew tremendously while mentoring them. They perceived that they were the ones being built up, but actually they did not realize that they were building me up without even realizing it.

It is essential to build a person to understand their impact on others, and build a drive to help others. This servant attitude is win-win. When we mentor people, we have an expectation that they too will begin to mentor others when they are ready.

An example of a person who had a focus on others even when he went through the roughest of times, is a man named Joseph in the

Bible. We can draw out a lot of mentoring lessons. Joseph was a very talented person. He had gone through a lot. His twelve brothers had always been very jealous of Joseph in large part due to his dad Jacob's favoring him over his brothers. His brother sold him into slavery when he was young, and then lied to his dad saying he had been mauled and killed by an animal.

Everything Joseph touched seemed to turn to gold. He is known for having favor with God. Because of this, Potiphar, who was an Egyptian officer of the Pharaoh, elected to put Joseph in charge of his household. Even though Joseph was a slave, he always maintained a positive attitude and always seemed to be put into a position in which he had an impact on those around him.

Joseph was incredibly loyal. He was said to be very good looking and muscular. He had all of the opportunity to be arrogant and think he was better than everyone else, yet he did not. He was a humble person who was always focused on doing what is right rather than complain that he had been wronged.

Potiphar's wife became attracted to Joseph and did everything she could to seduce him, but she continually failed. Joseph even went so far as to admonish her that he would never betray the trust placed in him by Potiphar. Of course she did not take no for an answer. She was used to getting what she wanted. On one occasion, Joseph was left all alone in the house with Potiphar's wife. The other slaves were nowhere to be found. They quite possibly could have been sent out for a task so she could make Joseph vulnerable. She began to seduce Joseph again, but he refused, and actually began to run from her. She grabbed his shirt, and as he pulled away, his shirt came off. This woman was so angry at Joseph. How dared he think he could refuse her!

When her husband Potiphar came home, because of her anger, she falsely accused Joseph of rape. Potiphar had Joseph immediately jailed. Imagine that, being put in jail by the very person you were trying to remain loyal to.

While in jail, Joseph again began to do well. His ability to influence those around him was incredible. He became a favorite of the Warden, and was then put in charge of all the prisoners. Later Joseph interpreted dreams and was released and made to be Pharaoh's right-hand man. The bottom line was that Joseph had every reason to feel sorry for himself, yet he never did. He always made the best of every circumstance. Instead of being focused on his circumstances, he would focus on those around him and how he could impact those around him for good. By doing that, he had much fruit from his labor.

An individual that reminds me of Joseph is Lalo Gunther. I arrested Lalo a few times and began to try and mentor him when he was about fourteen years old. Lalo had a rough family life and no father. He basically ran amok whenever he wanted to. Eventually, he was locked up for several years in the California Youth Authority. He had a tough time being incarcerated, yet he always was impacting those around him for the good and had favor from the warden. He was assigned the position of Wards Rights Specialist, which gave him even more credibility and access to the other prisoners whom Lalo was trying to impact. Here is his story from his perspective …

The Lalo Gunther Story

My story begins at the time I was about five years old. It was during this time that I found myself lacking. There was a real need inside of me to feel cared for, loved and believed in. I can vividly remember a time when I was acting out in order to get attention. I was so frustrated as a little boy because I was not receiving the attention I so needed. My mother was doing her normal shouting-at-me routine which only escalated my hurt feelings and fueled more outbursts. Her boyfriend was there at this time, and he saw something that neither my mother nor I could have., He said to my mother, "All Lalo wants is for you to hold him and kiss him and tell him you love him." I could not believe he said that, but before I could respond with more outbursts it pierced me like a knife. I can still feel that event today as I think about it. I stood there almost motionless, but I felt that this guy was right and wanted so desperately for my mother to reach over and just hold me. Instead, she just reacted defensively and said, "*El sabe que yo lo quero mucho.*" In English she was saying that "He knows that I care for him a lot." Inside myself I wondered how much she really did care.

Throughout my childhood and on into my teen years, I would recount the number of times I had been let down and disappointed by different adults and peers who had come into my life. When I was age two, my parents split up, and I would only see my biological father every now and then. To this day he has never attempted to be a father to me; instead, the small amount of time that I have had a chance to be around him, his attempt is to be more of a friend or acquaintance. I desperately wanted an adult to be there for me and invest in me. I so longed to have someone there for me to take me fishing, to a ball game or just sit and tell me about life. Instead, I grew up on the street; I learned how to be a "man" on the street. There was no one willing to stand up and be a father figure to me in my neediest of times. It was so difficult at times to cope with this, in school I felt so inadequate, almost stupid because I didn't know as much as the next kid. All through my elementary years I lacked a male role model.

During my junior high years I began to either gain a little confidence or really not understand who I was or who I wanted to be. Either way, I began to land myself in a whole lot of trouble. It was as if I were seeking out my own identity. I really didn't have a true self-identity; at this point I only did what others did. I was desperately seeking to be a part of something that I felt was meaningful. Throughout this time there were different teachers and counselors whom I respected and liked, but they all left me hanging. I wanted them to really care about who I was, but it felt like they didn't.

In the later part of my junior high years, I was sent to live with some friends of my family. This family gave me many things, but it felt inadequate for what I searched for. The emptiness in my heart still remained. After eight months, I was kicked out of their home and sent back to live with my mom and siblings. This is where my life would take a somewhat different path.

My life back home was different, as I had been gone for enough time to be uncomfortable with the way things were. The family I had remembered in the past was  now complete without me, but here I was. My desire was to be a part of something that mattered; I wanted to have some purpose for my life. At this point there was a group of people my age that belonged to a gang. I would observe these individuals every time I left or arrived at my apartment complex. I never really knew what they all had in common, but I would think to myself, "I wish I had a lot of friends like that."

The place where I lived was on a street that had mostly apartments on it. Police cars would drive by at least a few times a day; it seemed like there was always some type of problem. Outside of my apartment, there were always some gang members. No matter if it was daytime or nighttime, gang members were always outside. The window in our living room apartment faced the street and so I could see at all times what was transpiring outside.

In my last junior high year, I had gotten myself in trouble with a local family of Chaldeans (who had immigrated from Iraq), and there was going to be a fight after school at the local park. I only had about two friends who were going to back me up, but the Chaldeans brought their whole family for the fight. As I arrived at the park, I noticed a few of the gang members hanging out on my street. One of them saw what was transpiring and said he would back me up. I didn't really know him, but the offer seemed too good to turn down. This would open the door for me to get to know these gang members. It seemed like overnight I began to make friends with these gang members, and before long I was with them day in and day out.

This was all new to me, hanging out with a group of people who all shared a common bond. It seemed as if they all cared for each other, and I was feeling the "love" that I wanted from my family, which I failed to receive from my father or my mother. My involvement in the gang lifestyle continued to progress and led me into a darker hole than before.

It had been less than a year, and at the age of fifteen I found myself in juvenile hall, and this was only the beginning. During this time I also was kicked out of the local high school I was supposed to be attending. This resulted in my being sent to a continuation school, at which a miracle occurred. At the disciplinary continuation school where I found myself, a police officer had been assigned. This part of my story began what I call the "mentoring years."

At the age of fifteen, after joining a gang, being kicked out of school, being placed on probation, I meet a police officer. I remember the day as if it were yesterday, during a passing period in the morning. I was on my way to one of my classes with one of my friends they called Topo. Topo knew this cop, whose name I would later find out was Kevin. They began to talk, and then the cop wanted to know who I was. Of course there was no way in the world I wanted to get to know this cop, and especially for him to know who I was. So when he asked who I was, I just turned around and walked the other way.

For some reason I would see this cop in many different places. Not only was he the police officer assigned to my school, but also he was the police officer assigned to the gang detail for the entire city of El Cajon. As I hung out with my friends in front of my apartment complex, this police officer would drive by. On more than one occasion he would stop and began to attempt to talk with us. My feelings were the same; I wanted nothing to do with a cop. Before long he knew who I was and would attempt to talk with me every time he would come into contact with me.

Kevin had made a name for himself in El Cajon; as I would soon find out, almost all of the gang members knew who he was. I was shocked. Some of the guys with whom I hung around would even go on outings with this police officer, leaving me even more shocked. Then a friend of mine suggested we go to a Bible study with this cop. I was very skeptical, but because my friend said there would be pretty girls there, I agreed to go. That night is also very memorable to me; I remember the ride back to our city in this cop's white Ford Ranger pick up truck with a camper shell. I rode in the back on our way to the study and on the way back I decided I would ride in the front. To get under this guy's skin, I would play some of "our" music. I asked him if I could, and he said yes, so I gave him one of our tapes. We played "Eighteen with a Bullet," the gangster version. When the song got to the expletives, I just watched his expression—nothing. However, after that song was over, Kevin decided he had had enough of this stuff and said it was time for his music. I have to admit I respected him for allowing me to play my music even though he disapproved, and I knew it wasn't good stuff.

Before I could even figure out what was happening, I would be routinely hanging out with this guy. I began attending the Bible studies, pizza nights, adventuresome outings and even church with this guy. My heart began to open up to Kevin, but I couldn't totally figure him out. Slowly, I began to understand where he was coming from. We would have many long talks and some very emotional dialogues. He would strongly attempt to pull out of me what I wanted for my future. I would try to come up with an answer, but I didn't really know. My life was moving so fast and I was trying to figure things out, but life was cloudy and I couldn't even see beyond the next step.

I have to say that this man was showing me and giving me what I never had. Many times I would share my heart with him and find myself in tears. I didn't cry; that wasn't me and I had no reason to.

But this guy would touch chords in my heart that I had kept locked since childhood. Since the time my mom locked her emotions away from me, it had been painful to open the door to my heart. For some reason I felt safe with this guy; he truly demonstrated what I had lacked in my life.

Even though there were great times of growth in our relationship and my life, I still had a propensity to be a gang member and loved the fact that the gang stood together. On one occasion, Kevin came to my house, arrested me, and took me to juvenile hall. I knew I deserved it, but for him it seemed very difficult to book me in. This showed me another side of him. He would write to me, even come in and lead Bible studies for the inmates inside of juvenile hall. He would visit me and again re-ignite that emotional discourse that we shared. No matter where I was, Kevin stood by my side more than anyone ever had in my life.

It was hard sometimes to understand our relationship. My peers would always made fun of me, saying things like, "Where's your dad LaChapelle?" This would tick me off. In reality he was slowly filling that role in my life, but I was going to fight before I would ever admit that. This long-term friendship would continue to be molded into something for the future. On several occasions Kevin met me at the El Cajon Police Department. This experience was anything but pleasant. I remember entering the station, a place that I had been brought to many times when I was arrested. I would come in with my usual gang member dress style, and I would ask to see Officer LaChapelle. I always wondered what the officers would think about this hoodlum who had been here under different circumstances now coming to the station asking for Kevin. Kevin sometimes would have one of the officers let me in and go back and meet him. I would walk through the station and exit just as the off duty officers did. Weird!

So many different things penetrated my heart. On another occasion I went to the movies with Kevin. As we sat in the theater, he asked if I wanted some popcorn, and I replied, sure. He then handed me his wallet and asked me to go and purchase the popcorn. I felt almost fearful carrying around a cop's wallet; it was all intact with money and his police identification card. I also attended an award banquet for the El Cajon Police Department at the Elks Club. As I and about ten other gang members entered the room, I felt we were in the wrong place, but when Kevin received his award we all went to the front and stood by his side for pictures. Things like this change your way of thinking; it really gives you a deeper perspective on people and who they are.

As the years went by I realized more and more that this guy Kevin cared for me in a true way, and that my gang cared for me less and less. My time of change, however, would not come until the year 1995, four years after I met Kevin. Everything he taught me, the way in which he was there for me, would not easily be forgotten. On June 9, 1995, I was arrested and charged with attempted murder, and the reality of it all was about to hit me.

I had just been released from serving eight months in a juvenile camp and had told Kevin that when I was released, I wanted to do good. I lied to Kevin about my release date, and it hadn't been two hours before one of my friends picked me up from the bus station. I then cruised down the street with a bandana on my head, and as Kevin was eating lunch at a nearby restaurant, he looked up and recognized me. I was out for three months. I wanted to do well, but again I found myself with my old friends. I wanted to be someone else so bad that the week before I was arrested, I knelt down at the end of my bed and with tears in my eyes, I asked God to allow something major to happen to me to get my attention, maybe even that I would be arrested for something big, and hopefully this would wake me up.

As that prayer was answered faster than I would realize, I found myself in a maximum security cell all by myself. My whole world crumbled around me; it was now time to change the course of my life. Kevin had been working on a project out of the country when all of this went down. When he returned to find out my situation, he was devastated. He let me know in letters how disappointed he was with me, but for some reason said he still loved me and would be there for me. My mom visited me and expressed the same sentiment. I just let the tears flow down my face as I realized how bad this was. The District Attorney was going to make an example out of me and was going to take me all the way to trial with no plea bargain. His goal was to see me get life in prison. I soon understood this was very serious and that I might never be getting out again.

While my world came crashing down, I thought a lot about my family and how I was never there for them. Two smaller brothers and two smaller sisters with no dad at home, just an older brother who should have been looking out for them and instead had been consumed with himself and trapped in his own world. I was so sickened that I had forsaken my role as a protector to them and now was on my way to cementing that reality. I had twenty-two hours a day to just sit and think about all this. I was only allowed out of my cell for two hours a day. What could I do at this point to make my life count for something? I read my Bible. One night, the wrestling in my heart had come to a breaking point. I had decided that my family and those who really cared for me were more important than I or my present situation was. I remember looking out my little five-inch window to the sky and I said to God, "If you are real, change my life, change my heart, I want to be a different person." That night was one of the most emotional nights of my life. I cried like a baby, and for the next couple of months I shed tears as the God of love would pour out His presence to me. Instead of being at odds with Kevin, I was now becoming a team member with Kevin.

Although was convicted of a felony on this case, I later was able to have my record sealed by the court.

Quickly I began to have his heart for wanting to help others. We would tag team on sharing with people that there was more to life. Many people like me had lived life for themselves and had hurt those who really cared for them. The seeds that Kevin had shared with me in the past were now beginning to blossom. Kevin was the one who taught me to say 'I love you' to those around us. Up until this time, I never told any of my brothers or sisters or even my mom that I loved them. Slowly that began to change. I remember that Kevin would always tell me he loved me and I would just think, "Yeah, whatever." But as a kid who had never heard this before, it broke through the strongholds I had placed around my heart.

I sit back and just want Kevin to know that I love him and recognize that he did not have to invest his time, talent and treasure into my life. I will never be able to repay him for all he has done and all he has meant to me throughout my life. I also ask him to forgive me for all the wrongs I have caused in his life.

It has been twelve years now since the time of this life-changing experience and in retrospect many things come to mind. I would exhort those like Kevin to continue to press on and not give up believing in the people they mentor. It took me close to four years to learn and understand and want to change. I put Kevin through an emotional time consuming roller-coaster, but thanks to his persistence I  am who I am today. Words cannot express the gratitude of emotion I feel for Kevin and for him not giving up on me. Individuals that grow up in similar situations as myself, lack many things, but by believing in them you allow them to discover their maximum potential and turn it into a reality. I am thankful for Kevin's dedication! I am so thankful for my wife Dara who God blessed me with.

Mentoring For Success

There are a few other incredible individuals whom I have had the honor of mentoring over the years who have become like family to me. They continue to have the most profound impact on my life. The most incredible attribute each of these individuals now carries is the burden to mentor others.

One individual is Sion Brannan. Sion's friendship has been incredible, especially over the past few years. Sion, now in his thirties, was only fifteen years old when our paths crossed. He was heavily entrenched into the gang culture. He endured a lot, including being the victim of a shooting that nearly killed him when he was eighteen years old. His mother and I encouraged him to  leave San Diego and start over. Sion not only started over but earned his Bachelor of Science degree in Mathematics at Cal Poly. He then went on to obtain his teaching credential, and taught high school for a few years in San Jose, California. Recently, Sion joined the U.S. Army as a Second Lieutenant to serve his Country. Sion has persevered against great odds to succeed in his life as well as in his career.

Sion and I have enjoyed an incredibly close relationship even though we are hundreds of miles apart from each other. Sion seems to know exactly how I am thinking, and we are like-minded in so many ways, it is crazy. Recently, Sion and I put a video documentary together about his life. It was very emotional for the both of us to look back and reflect on all we had been through together. It scares me knowing that Sion's chosen profession of being a military officer will place him in serious harm's way. I cannot imagine him losing his life, yet I respect and admire his courage and commitment to this country. Words cannot describe our friendship and the admiration and respect I have for him.

Another incredible friend is Luis Castillo and his wife Lucia who have mastered their role as loving and caring parents for their two children. Luis exemplifies his role as a husband and father while Lucia exemplifies her role as a wife and mother. Luis is so loyal to his family that many of his peers look to him as an example as to how they need to lead their own families. Luis, his wife and their children are a blessing to us all. Their genuine and consistent love for God and family stands out in a world where families are so often split apart. Luis has such a genuine heart, and is such a loyal friend.

David Rios became involved in our boxing program when he was fifteen years old back in about 1993. He had great talent and artistic ability. Over the years, our friendship has grown and never wavered. We have stood together through good times and bad. David and his wife Kat have two children. I can remember during rough times, David would put his arm around me and tell me everything would be okay. Man, did that mean a lot and carry me through some of the darkest times of my life.

I was very protective of the guys whom I was mentoring. I can remember a time when David showed up to our boxing club. His arm was swollen and appeared to have been broken. A bone was protruding from his arm like a compound fracture. I asked  David what had happened. He told me he fell. I did not believe it. I persuaded him to tell me the truth. He finally confided in me that while walking to practice, a group of gang members jumped him and ripped a gold chain with the letter "D" on it from his neck. His dad had given it to him as a gift. The "D" was for David. I was so angry. I knew how gentle David was and how forgiving he was. He kept telling me that it was okay, and that he forgave the guys. Well, I was not content with that. I loaded him in my vehicle to take him to the hospital. He had told me this happened near the El Cajon High School. I was already nearby, so I asked him that if he saw the guys while we were driving, to tell me. As I passed a group of El Cajon Dukes gang members whom I recognized, I saw David slouch down in the passenger seat. I could clearly sense that he was afraid, and these were the guys. I said, "David, are these the guys? Tell me the truth!" He said under his breath, "Yeah, those are the guys." I pulled over, jumped out and ordered all of the subjects to the ground and called for additional officers to assist me. We ended up arresting the group for strong-arm robbery. One of the guys, John Fratt, who had thrown a karate kick at David's arm, was charged with felony battery.

I remember later visiting juvenile hall and seeing the guys who had committed the crime. I talked with them and told them the kind of person David was and that David specifically asked me to tell them he offered his forgiveness. They actually cried when I told them that. They were convicted and sentenced. Here is a note from David on his view of Mentorship:

I met Kevin during the summer of 1993. I had just started the 10th grade. One day a friend told me that there was a boxing club not very far from school. He said it was a nice place. Since I was very much interested in boxing, I decided to check the place out. I was real excited because one of my biggest dreams was to join some sort of boxing organization.

That afternoon right after school I decided to check the place out and see if it was really all I heard it would be. I also liked the fact that the gym was only three blocks away from my house. The gym was so popular for the fact that it had such a different, and positive, atmosphere.

The first day I went, all my friends were there. As soon as I had entered the gym, I felt right at home. It was very clean, and the people that were in charge of organizing the gym were very friendly. Kevin was then introduced to me for the first time. I didn't know that he was a peace officer for the city of El Cajon, let alone that he planned out, set up, and ran the gym on a daily basis.

It was obvious to everyone that I had been there for the first time but there was something about the staff, their entire attitude and demeanor was so different and outgoing, that it was almost like something out of a book or movie. Kevin was a very gracious and caring person; something I didn't quite expect due to his being a police officer.

We had an awkward relationship at first, somewhat uncomfortable. He was very strict in the rules. It took a couple weeks, and I started to see things in a different way and I realize that this guy was serious about improving the community by actually doing something great for it. Not just the community but for us, who at the time were lost souls and considered outcasts by the rest of society and were looking for guidance and a positive role model in our lives.

The program, called Bridge the Gap at the time, will always hold a special place in my mind, just as the person who created it, will always have a special place in my heart. The next year Kevin was elected to the Grossmont Union High School District Board of Education. Being an elected official was not going to be an easy task. But in my mind I knew that he was going to give his best effort for he is not a man who would start something and live it half-way through. That's not the friend I know. He is a man who is very determined in what he believes.

He thought that the students needed more than what we were already learning. During his time on the board, he was going to look into the most important things for students and not just administration. Therefore, he thought that something needed to be done. At first it seems funny knowing that he was going to be running for the school board because I thought he was joking about it and was not being serious. I later realized that he meant business.

When he was elected, I was very happy. That was another triumph for him and at the same time a great example for all of us. He was one of the greatest role models I have ever known in my entire life, and he still is. During his four years on the school board, he went through a lot of stressful times. There were sometimes when he wanted to give up and forget about the whole thing and not be part of it. He realized that during his most painful situations he was never left alone for there always was someone whom he could count on, his very best friends. It is interesting that when I first met Kevin, I did not like his strict attitude. Later, we became best of friends, as we still are today.

Kevin has accomplished many things and still more things to come. He has true faith in God. Over the years I have been able to share the deepest things with Kevin. Never did he reject me or look down on me; he stood at my side and helped me through the low times in my life. He also trusted me with very deep things. Our sharing bonded our friendship like never before. Having said all this, I know that he doesn't hear this much, but all I want to say is that I love him so much and I'm thankful to God for having given me a friend like Kevin M. LaChapelle.

Raul and Leti Flores and their two children are an incredible family. I met Raul when he was involved in a fight. He was about 14 years old and just dabbling in the gang scene. One day I met with his family to discuss my concerns over his behavior. I found his parents to be very responsive to my concerns. They decided to  move Raul back to Tecate, Mexico. His family invited me to Tecate, Mexico, and this is what set my heart on fire for the Country of Mexico. Raul is now in his thirties, married with two children, and he and his wife own and operate a pharmacy in Tecate. They are best friends, and it shows in the family they are raising. It is a blessing to see the fruits of their labor. They recently completed building their new home. Raul is so full of business savy and wisdom from his father. They consider me part of their family, and I consider them a part of mine.

It is absolutely amazing how many individuals I have seen first-hand drastically change the direction of their lives, many of whom did so against great odds! If I had to come up with a theme for the experiences I have witnessed over the years, I would have to say it is seeing people bring out the best in each other. Watching individuals struggling in their lives, and then when the light comes on and they are on the right track, they pass on what they have learned by mentoring others as well. By mentoring one young person at a time, that person is changed, and then will go on to change the lives of others. Like the rippling affect in a pond, the positive effects of PowerMentor continue making a difference in the future of troubled young people everywhere.

It is incredible when I sit back and reflect with guys whom I have mentored over the past twenty years. Watching them make decisions in their lives, and mentoring others, including their own children, often brings tears of joy to my eyes. We walk through life together helping each other overcome weaknesses, while helping each other maximize our effectiveness to meet the challenge of the mission placed upon our lives.

CHAPTER 11

▼

NEVER GIVE UP ON OTHERS

Never ever think of giving up on your mentee. We as mentors must encourage each other. We are all in the trenches together, and at times we get discouraged when we do not see progress with our mentees. I received an email from a school counselor in Turlock, California. She emailed to thank PowerMentor.org for the encouragement she received while visiting our website. She told of the impact it had on her. She is a counselor at a continuation high school working with at-risk young people who do not have a positive family model. She knows that by believing in them, they can do great things. She shared how difficult it is at times because she believes so much in the students and she wants them to do well, but often they give up because they don't believe in themselves. She goes home emotionally drained from what she hears them tell her about their home lives, and that they do not believe in themselves. Sometimes, this counselor wonders if she is making a difference. When she saw the video documentaries on our website sharing success stories of individuals, she said it greatly inspired and encouraged her.

I have the privilege of seeing years and years of planting seeds, and now watching these once at-risk young people walk through life as productive adults, impacting anyone they can find. This counselor can never forget that her words of encouragement, her believing in them, will never be in vain. She may not see the fruit immediately, but she is an integral part of a greater plan in helping a person find their purpose and meaning for their life.

This counselor also commented that sometimes she talks to young people and doesn't know if they are listening or believing what she is saying about the greatness that lies within them, and she wonders if her words are even helping! She reflected on our success story videos, which helped her to understand she is and will continue to make a difference impacting the students at her school. She said, "I tell God that I know I might not see the fruit for years, but I will still plant seeds in the lives of these young people, especially in light of the fact that no one else is, and many people have already given up on them." She refuses to give up on her students!

Here is the perspective from a student who was impacted by his high school teacher. Ryan Gunther, is the brother of Lalo Gunther. Ryan shares what his teacher Mrs. Martinez did for him:

Ryan's Story

A mentor, to me, is someone who dramatically changes the course of someone's life. It's someone who helps you when you're lost; someone who guides you to the light at the end of the tunnel.

Growing up for me wasn't easy with only one parent. I never met my father and having a family with five kids would be difficult for any mother, let alone the kids. My mother worked to keep up with the bills and to put food on the table. She didn't have much time to be around us kids. The only thing I had going for me was school. Going to school for me was just a typical day like it is for any kid growing up. School wasn't something I really thought was important. It was just a place where I had to go and where I could hang out with my friends. I was able to pick up things quickly but never really put those things I learned into practice, so I was an average student. I never really got the push from anyone to excel in school. No one ever told me that it was important for my future. My mother didn't go to school beyond middle school, and I looked up to her and thought to myself, "It must not be that important if she didn't go to school." She tried to tell me to do the best I could. But even if I didn't do well, she wouldn't be able to tell the difference because she couldn't understand, so I never tried. When I needed help I had no one to go to so it made no difference to me how I did in school. It didn't help that I was quiet and never asked for help from anyone when I didn't understand. It was like that for me up until my last year of middle school.

My last year of middle school I was placed into a program called AVID, which I only agreed to because most of my friends were taking it. AVID was an acronym for "Advancement Via Individual Determination." Those words would impact me more than I ever thought possible. AVID prepped me for college and its expectations. It taught me how to reach my potential in education. The things I learned didn't sink into my roots until I reached high school. The program there was more advanced, and the teacher was nothing short of a hero/mentor. She instilled in me this drive to make the best of every opportunity given to me, whether it be sports, educational or personal. It was more the story of her success that instilled in me the desire to set goals for my life. She preached that getting an education was important if you wanted to be successful in life; that it was the only practical thing that everyone could do if they wanted to. This was nothing I hadn't heard before, but Mrs. Martinez, my AVID teacher in high school, had lived out what she was talking about. She wasn't just simply saying it because it was her job. She's the only one in her family that went to college and excelled in it. For the first time in my life, I paid attention to someone who was trying to tell me the importance of education. It didn't just simply pass by me like the other times teachers had told me the same thing. She truly cared about her students, and the things she would say were solid. I can recall one time in class in which these kids were laughing at a girl who had a strong English accent. She was pronouncing a word kind of funny, and every time she said it, the kids would laugh. The girl caught on that they were laughing at her, and she ran out of the class crying. Mrs. Martinez went after her and when they came back they both came in with tears on their faces. Her shedding tears with her student had profound impact on me. She really cared about her students, and that made all the difference for me to follow her lead.

I wanted to be the first in my family to get a college education, the first one to go to a four year university, just like her. She opened the door for me to the world of college. She was the one pushing me to look for scholarships and taking the SAT, and the one telling me to apply for colleges my senior year. Before I was accepted into AVID, my grades were average. My grade point average was usually 2.7 GPA, but after being taught the AVID approach to learning, my grade point average raised one full point to 3.7 GPA. There were a couple of semesters in which I nearly obtained a 4.0 GPA. Never had I imagined that I would one day be earning grades like that.

The time finally came for students to begin to receive their letters from colleges and find out if they were accepted or not. Sometime in May I received my first letter from one of the schools I had applied to. I sat there holding it in my hand; it was from San Diego State University. I was scared to open it; all that I was striving for and worked for depended on this letter. Was I accepted or not? I finally opened it and read, "Dear Ryan Gunther, We are glad to inform you that you have been accepted to attend San Diego State University …" As I realized the results, tears began to trickle down my face. I had done it. My dream of going to a four-year university had come true.

I owe my success to Mrs. Martinez for opening my eyes to something bigger than I had ever imagined. It is people like this that are heroes to so many people out there who just need that push, that guidance and that power to excel in life. I would like to thank her and those who devote the countless hours of their lives to bringing hope to someone who may need it. It's a priceless act that few are able to commit to. That, to me, is the power to mentor.

Ryan's story is so indicative of the many young people whom I have seen mentored over the years that had a very poor self image, and had no vision for their lives. They had been conditioned over the years to limit themselves, not even knowing why. It reminds me of a story of a scientific study which was conducted. Five monkeys were placed in a cage. A banana was hung from the top of the cage. Anytime a monkey would try to climb up and grab the banana, the handlers would spray the monkey with water. After a very short amount of time, none of the monkeys would even consider climbing up to get the banana. Time went on, and one monkey at a time would be replaced with a new monkey. The new monkey would follow the established behavior pattern, not even once trying to climb up to get the banana. Pretty soon, all of the monkeys had been replaced, leaving not one original monkey who had witnessed the water being sprayed at any monkey trying to grab the banana. No monkey would try and get the banana. They probably did not even know why, just that no other monkey climbed up to get the banana, so it must be off limits for them too. Often times we are put in circumstances in which we are led to believe that we are just not cut out for college. Everyone around me drops out of school, gets a job, and that is their life. Little do they know that there is a greater plan for them to reach up for that banana; however, they do not even know why they do not reach up for it, they have merely been conditioned to accept the fact that college is off limits.

Another story also sheds light on our limiting ourselves and each other. If you were to place some fleas into a glass jar and place a lid on the jar, after some time, even if the lid were removed, the fleas would not try to fly out because they have placed an artificial ceiling upon themselves. The lid is gone, yet they still think it is in place. The same goes for mentoring young people. As barriers begin to be removed, it is hard for them to realize the barrier is no longer present. It takes time for them to take some baby steps of faith.

At times our mentees hold themselves hostage with the issues that they will not let go of, and their holding traps themselves. A final story that illustrates this well is how monkeys are caught in parts of Asia. A strong wooden box is fastened to a solid tree with a chain. A small hole is drilled in the box allowing the hand of the monkey to barely fit through. The trapper places nuts or fruit inside the box and leaves it overnight. A monkey comes along smelling the fruit or nuts. The monkey sticks his hand into the hole, grabbing the food inside. The monkey then is not able to pull its hand back out of the hole because it has gripped the food with its hand. If the monkey would simply let go of the food, his hand would slip right out of the hole; however, the monkey will not let go. All night long, the monkey will try hard to get his hand out of the hole without letting go of the food that initially tempted the monkey in the first place. Again, if the monkey would just let go, it would free itself, but instead has trapped itself. Often mentees will not let go of the very think that is destroying their life or their goals. They hang on and hang on until they finally realize they are trapped. Often the monkey scars its wrist from trying to pull so hard, instead of just letting go of the food and simply slipping its hand right out.

We, the mentors, are the ones watching the mentee refuse to let go of things that are trapping their lives, yet all we can do is gently help them understand that they just need to let go. Likewise, there are times we need to let go of our mentees. Maybe our time is done, and there will be another person brought into their life to plant seeds. However, we stunt their growth because we won't let go of them. We want them to let us control their lives, yet we cannot!

So as a mentor, we have to let go, but at the same time, we can never ever give up on our mentee! You have experiences and knowledge that only you can offer to those around you. We all bring different strengths to the table. Understand how much impact you have. Focus your talent by creating a personal mission statement along with core values. In creating your personal mission statement, consider what others know you for. Do they know you for your encouragement, your wisdom, your loyalty, tenacity, or what? If you do not know, ask your closest friends how they see you? Ask them what talent they see within you? Consider sending out an email to your friends with a brief survey.

The next step is to put together a mission statement of two or three sentences for your life. This is crucial because when you encounter times of discouragement or a lack of focus, you can always go back to your personal mission statement as an anchor. For example, my personal mission statement is:

Changing lives, one person at a time through
Motivation, inspiration, and having a positive impact,
Helping others to recognize their God given purpose and ability.

I also recommend you make a wallet card of your mission statement that you carry with you. For example, I have a group photo of a hiking trip which is very meaningful to me. I have added my mission statement to the image and printed it out for my wallet card. I then find an opportunity to ask others what their mission in life is and show them my mission wallet card. It really holds you accountable for your mission. Never forget the impact you will have on those around you.

We would like to be a resource for you as well. Visit us at www.powermentor.org if we can ever be of assistance to you or if you would like to book us for speaking engagement.

AFTERWORD

The greatest asset a person can have is the unfailing commitment from a mentor. A true mentor walks alongside their mentee believing in them, all the while offering straightforward advice. In addition, the mentor should provide a support system to their mentee which is composed of providing discipline on the one hand, and a nurturing influence on the other. Replicating an intact family unit can be underestimated. The functional family is by far the best support system for an individual. But again, because the family has failed so many, we must improvise and mirror this support to try and build up individuals who were not so fortunate to have a functional family.

One last story should give you insight as to the crisis many young people find themselves in due to their parents living for themselves instead of for their children. Two young brothers who are absolutely incredible and have phenomenal potential are Rudy and Kike. Any parent would be so proud of these guys. Unfortunately, their dad abandoned them when they were young, and their mother lives on the streets with a drug problem. These two have bounced around from relative to relative. Imagine what they feel, the rejection, the loneliness, the fear of walking through life. We at PowerMentor are committed to seeing them through their life. These two guys are so incredible. We see the greatness in them, and can see clearly where God will take them in their lives. It is an exciting adventure through life to walk alongside these two, and watch how they are molded and made for a greater purpose! I tell them how I consider them to be family, because they are.

Never give up on your mentee. You may not see the fruit of your labor for years to come. Be steadfast in your mentoring and you will see results! Again, do not forget some of the nuggets of truth you have gleaned from reading this book. Especially do not forget to focus on what is right in people rather than what is wrong. If we continue to build what is going right in their lives, we will find that what is going wrong will slowly dissipate over time.

978-0-595-49666-2
0-595-49666-0

Printed in the United States
202471BV00001B/253-357/P